Liberating Ministry
from the Success Syndrome

Liberating
Ministry
from the
SUCCESS
SYNDROME

Kent and Barbara Hughes

Tyndale House Publishers, Inc.
Wheaton, Illinois

Scripture quotations marked NASB are from New
American Standard Bible, copyright 1960, 1962,
1963, 1971, 1973 by the Lockman Foundation.
Other Scripture quotations are from the Holy Bible,
New International Version. Copyright © 1973, 1978,
1984 International Bible Society. Used by permission
of Zondervan Bible Publishers.

Library of Congress Catalog Card Number 87-51463
ISBN 0-8423-2851-3, trade cloth
ISBN 0-8423-2849-1, trade paper special edition
Copyright 1987 by R. Kent and Barbara Hughes
All rights reserved
Printed in the United States of America
3   4   5   6   7   8   9   93   92   91   90   89

In memory of
Joe Bayly
and for
Mary Lou

CONTENTS

INTRODUCTION

Some onlookers thought it was unusual, but few noticed when the pastor wheeled into the church parking lot in a borrowed pickup truck. But everyone's eyes were upon him when he backed the truck across the lawn to his study door. Refusing comment or assistance, he began to empty his office onto the truck bed. He was impassive and systematic: first the desk drawers, then the files, and last his library of books, which he tossed carelessly into a heap, many of them flopping askew like slain birds. His task done, the pastor left the church and, as was later learned, drove some miles to the city dump where he committed everything to the waiting garbage.

It was his way of putting behind him the overwhelming sense of failure and loss that he had experienced in the ministry. This young, gifted pastor was determined never to return to the ministry. Indeed, he never did.

We wrote this book because of this story—and many, too many, others like it. We are concerned about the morale and survival of those in Christian ministry. Pastors, youth workers, evangelists, Sunday school teachers, lay ministers, missionaries, Bible study leaders, Christian writers and speakers, and those in other areas of Christian service often face significant feelings of failure, usually fueled by misguided expectations for success.

It is true that our Christian colleges, universities, and

seminaries are flooded annually with bright and motivated students. But it is also true that every year thousands leave the ministry convinced they are failures, seduced by what William James piquantly called "the bitch goddess of success."[1]

We know what it's like. We too almost succumbed to her enticements. It is our hope that the account of our subtle confusion about success, our near ruin, and ultimately our liberation through the truth of God's Word will aid in delivering others from this unhappy goddess.

This book is an effort to encourage those in ministry. It is our gift to our fellow servants.

We trust these thoughts will help you cope with the despair of failure, which we all face in God's work, and lead you to a deeper, fuller understanding of success in your ministry.

KENT AND BARBARA HUGHES

PART ONE

A DARK NIGHT OF THE SOUL

A Dark Night of the Soul

ONE

Disappointed Dreams

As I begin our story, do not suppose that this is the hardest thing that has happened to me in the ministry. It is not. The significance of my experience is not its hardness, but that it almost made me quit my divine calling.

When a man is forty-five he is said to be in mid-life, and I certainly am. It is also often said that he is in his prime, and that I am. I have been married twenty-five years to a woman who is not only my love but my soul partner. We have four children, all of whom love Christ and want to serve him in their callings.

Twenty-three of our twenty-five years have been spent in ministry. Preaching is my passion. Even on vacation, I enjoy books that have to do with the history of preaching and homiletic thought and theology. I feel as if I am doing the thing I was born for.

The ministry has made it possible for me to experience what some would (unwisely!) call success, as I have traveled widely, spoken to international conferences, written several books, and sat on the boards of Christian organizations.

Those who have served alongside me these past twenty-plus years say that they see me as a capable, solid, even-dispositioned pastor who has a positive approach to ministry—and all of life. And without hesitation I can say that they are right. Though I am not unfamiliar with dark moods, such times are rare in my life—and always have been.

All of this is what makes the following account so enlightening.

I was not feeling well as I stepped from the car onto my broiling southern California driveway and walked, briefcase in hand, toward the shade of the front porch. There Barbara cheerfully greeted me through the kitchen screen.

Aware of my gradual depression, she had been observing me with increasing concern. My gait had lost its characteristic energy and I often appeared downcast. Barbara knew that it had to do with my work, for she observed that when things were going well at church I was OK, but otherwise I was discouraged. If church attendance was up, I was up; if it was down, so was I. And the numbers had been going down for a long time.

What Barbara didn't know was that I was seriously wondering whether I should continue in the pastoral ministry. Neither was she aware that the doubts troubling me were actually so repugnant that I could not bring myself to verbalize them. Nor could she know that as I further suppressed them, my depression itself had become increasingly ugly.

A covert, unarticulated animosity had crept through my soul. It was hidden from all. Years of honestly cultivated Christian civility served me well—for inside I was a very angry man.

The focus of my resentment was God himself, the one who had called me to this. I had given *everything*—all my time, all my education, years of ministry and true Christian devotion (he knew!)—and now I was failing. God was to blame.

Beneath my pastoral veneer, dark thoughts moved at will.

Inside I was embarrassed and fearful. At night, as I drifted off to sleep, the beneficent faces of my well-wishers would slip in and out of focus—always smiling. They seemed benignly to watch me sink into a pit of miserable despair.

I wanted to quit.

How had I come to this? In retrospect, I can now see that much of it had to do with my *expectations*, which went back to the very week when as a twelve-year-old I met Christ at summer camp. . . .

I can still remember the glowing lens of my flashlight illuminating the delicate pages of my tiny Bible. After lights out, in the musty, gym-sock air of my sleeping bag, trembling with joy, I read and reread the great texts of salvation. I had come to know Christ!

Although I was not quite a teenager, I knew that I was called to preach. So sure was I that the next day I let everyone know. When I went home, I announced it to my family and gave testimony to it before the whole church. It was a precocious announcement, but it was of God. The call was never to leave me. It gave profound direction to my young life. God had saved me and called me, and in my youthful egocentricity, *I assumed he was going to do great things through me.*

Because of this my teenage years were full and focused. I wholeheartedly entered into the life of my local southern California high school and church—all the while happily growing in my pastor-to-be persona.

When just sixteen I preached my first sermon on Jonah and the Whale. I gave it a double title: "The Chicken of the Sea, or God Has a Whale of a Plan for Your Life!" So it was a sermon of dubious wit and doubtful quality! The mere doing of it established my identity as one called to the gospel ministry. Many kind and affirming people in my church predicted I would be a "good" preacher. And with their predictions, my anticipation of future success increased.

Despite my immature pride, my call was an intensely

serious matter to me. Virtually everything I did was with an expectant eye to the sacred goal of ministry.

I went to Whittier College. There I became deeply involved in studies and preparation for the pastorate. I directed Youth for Christ clubs, did some street preaching, and organized evangelistic outreaches to students at other colleges.

Meeting and marrying Barbara—my cheerful, outgoing, ministry-minded wife—deepened my commitment and the sense that the best times lay ahead.

Choosing to begin a family as college ended meant increased pressures. I attended classes, worked forty hours per week, and together Barbara and I began an exciting ministry with young married couples in our church that carried over into our years at nearby Talbot Theological Seminary. To be sure, our single-mindedness left us tired, but we were happy.

Seminary was all I had hoped for and more. There is a distinct romance to biblical study, "The Queen of Sciences," with its epic history, magisterial doctrines, delicately nuanced theology, its Greek and Hebrew. And I entered the romance completely, for studying the Scriptures and learning about Christ were heaven to me. Lifelong friendships with godly professors and students strengthened our resolve to serve God with all that we had. Seminary confirmed for me the rightness of my vocation. It also had the effect of heightening my expectations of success.

During seminary I began a memorable ten years of ministry in my family church, first as youth pastor and then as associate pastor. This was the sixties—restless, unsettled, but a time of wonderful spiritual harvest. Our Bible studies overflowed with teenagers honestly and earnestly seeking truth. Many not only met Christ but went on to become missionaries and ministers.

The highlight of that ministry is framed in a five-by-seven photograph hanging in the hallway of our home. The photo was taken in 1968 in Parker, Arizona, during our high schoolers' Easter Outreach week. It was snapped in the intense low morning sunlight of the Arizona desert, which gives it almost surrealistic detail. In the background is the turquoise ribbon of the morning-lit Colorado River. In the foreground are five young men posed on a boat trailer. They are tan, windswept, and holding beers with postured male élan. Three of those young men would confess Christ that morning. Today two of them are in the ministry and the other is now a prominent Christian counselor. That picture demonstrates for me the sovereign, ineluctable power of God. Those young men, before that week completely unknown to me, not only were revolutionized by God's grace but have led unusually productive Christian lives and have been my good friends for almost twenty years.

If only all of Christian ministry were as triumphant as that photograph. Unfortunately, ministry is messy. One experiences a wide range of disappointments and criticisms in ten years of aggressive Christian service.

Even so, those were productive and satisfying years. But, having reached the age of thirty-two, I realized it was time for me to begin an active pulpit ministry. God's call was clear. And I looked forward, with an anticipation that had been years in the making, to what God would do.

The church I served decided to mother a new church with me as the founding pastor. In this adventure, the sponsoring church and its pastor were wonderfully magnanimous. Together we produced an excellent multimedia presentation to communicate to the congregation the potential of the new work. When the pastor urged all to respond who felt the call of God to commit themselves to planting this new church, twenty families decided to go with us. To top that off, the church gave us a gift of $50,000 to get us started.

What a way to begin a church! Optimism ran high. As the fair-haired boy, I was told by friends that great things were about to happen, and it would not be long before the new church would be larger than its mother. Such talk enlarged my expectations. I believed it.

The people who gathered with us to begin the church were terrific. We left our initial meetings amazed at the array of gifted, hard-working, visionary people the Lord had brought with us. With such people we expected to grow.

And we did things "right." Our denomination retained a church growth expert who instructed us in the broad principles and minor subtleties of growing churches. They sent me to seminars on church growth. We obtained aerial photographs and demographic projections, commissioned ethnographic studies, consulted with the county, and chose the target community with painstaking and prayerful premeditation.

Beginning a new church is exhausting work, and we went for it with all we had. I found myself attending meetings, strategizing, canvassing, counseling, preparing sermons, and borrowing pianos, pianists, projectors, and pulpits. Then came the Sunday ritual of preparing the rented facilities for worship services—sweeping out the trash from the community center, helping Whitey Cary unload the big storage trailer containing the pulpit, microphones, hymnals, rugs, rockers, and playpens, and then in the evening working in happy Christian *bonhomie* with the entire congregation to disassemble and pack up our church for another week.

From the start, we had everything going for us. We had the prayers and predictions of our friends who believed a vast, growing work was inevitable. We had the sophisticated insights of the science of church growth. We had a superb nucleus of believers. And we had *me,* a young pastor with a good track record who was entering his prime. We expected to grow.

But to our astonishment and resounding disappointment, we didn't. In fact, after considerable time and incredible labor, we had fewer regular attenders than during the first six months. Our church was shrinking, and the prospects looked bad—really bad.

So as I walked up my driveway on this hot summer day in 1975, after more than a decade of ministry, I began to lose my equilibrium. My long-established world of bright prospects and success had melted around me.

I was in the darkest, deepest depression of my life. My memory of this time is of a gray, horizonless sea. A faint light falls from a threatening sky and I am treading water alone, sinking. Soon I will be below the surface. Melodramatic, to be sure! But that is how I felt. I wanted out.

Seeing Barbara's smile through the screen, I brightened, as always, and for the next few hours I was preoccupied with my happy young family. But after dinner, when the children were in bed, despondency crept over me once again.

Except for my wife, it seemed that no one cared. And on this hot summer's midnight of soul, I was ready to talk.

TWO

"Hang On to My Faith"

Late that night when the children were soundly sleeping and the only sound was that of insects flapping against the hot screens, I began to reveal the depth of my calamitous misery to Barbara. As I spoke, my eyes burned red with frustration and anger. Dark thoughts mounted within, waiting their escape.

Barbara's attempts to soothe me received predictable responses. When she said, "Honey, your sermon really spoke to me last week," I responded, "Yes, but I'll just be on trial again next week." Again, she tried to cheer me up. She said that in her study of Genesis she saw that Noah had preached for 120 years without a single convert. My dark-humored response was, "Yes, but there wasn't another Noah across town with people flowing into *his* ark!" Barbara was terribly frustrated too—and with obvious good reason. But unlike me, her faith did not waver. And on this hot September evening I poured out all my dammed-up, hidden feelings.

What came forth was repugnant and offensive—truly mean. "Most people I know in the ministry are unhappy," I said. "They are failures in their own eyes. Mine as well. Why should I expect God to bless me when it appears he hasn't blessed them? Am I so ego-centered to think he loves me more?"

I wasn't exaggerating the situation. Conversations over

the years at pastors' conferences supported my thoughts. A few moments of personal exchange with a pastor almost invariably revealed immense hurt and self-doubt. Most pastors were unhappy with themselves and their work. And I secretly agreed with many of their self-assessments.

I went on: "In cold statistics my chances of being a failure are overwhelming. Most pastors do little more than survive in the ministry in piddly little churches." I rehearsed how a professor had stood before my seminary class and said that eight out of ten will never pastor a church larger than 150 people. Those were the statistics. And if true, they condemned most pastors to subsistence living unless their wives worked outside the home. "The ministry is asking too much of me," I said to Barbara. "How can I go on giving all that I have without seeing results, especially when others are?" I had been working day and night with no visible return. Everyone needs to see results. Farmers see their crops grow. It is their proper reward. I could see others' "crops" grow, but my field bore nothing.

If not that, then how should I measure my success? "If I were in the business world," I thought aloud that night, "it would be measured by the size of my bank account. Life's successes are measured quantitatively. How can anyone be expected to do otherwise?

"Those who really make it in the ministry are those with exceptional gifts. If I had a great personality or natural charisma, if I had celebrity status, a deep resonant voice, a merciless executive ability, a domineering personality that doesn't mind sacrificing people for success, I could make it to the top. Where is God in all of this?" I defied Barbara to disprove me. "Just look at the great preachers today. Their success seems to have little to do with God's Spirit; they're just superior people!"

Suddenly I found myself coming to a conclusion that I didn't want to admit. Though I knew it had been brooding in me for quite some time, now it was finally coming out. "God has called me to do something he hasn't given me the gifts to accomplish. Therefore, God is not good."

There. Finally, I had blurted out the thought that had tormented me. It fell between us, ugly and misshapen, into the silence of the hot night. I knew I had been called by God; I had never been able to escape that call, nor had I wanted to. But now I felt that I was the butt of a cruel joke. I was a failure. I wanted to quit. And in aching desperation I said to my dear wife, "What am I to do?"

How distressing it must have been for Barbara. I had always been the one on whom she could depend—and I was faltering. But I will never forget her kind and confident response. "I don't know what you're going to do. But for right now, for tonight, hang on to my faith. Because I believe. I believe that God is good. I believe that he loves us and is going to work through this experience. So hang on to my faith. I have enough for both of us."

That night I went to bed exhausted. Barbara stayed up long into the morning hours reflecting on our conversation.

"Hang on to my faith." Had I really spoken those words to Kent only a few minutes earlier? Sitting alone at the kitchen table, I wondered now if I had simply been mouthing pious bravado.

What about my faith? Was it strong enough to survive on its own or had Kent married a spiritual dependent? If Kent's faith failed, would mine shrivel and die like a parasite separated from its host?

My earliest recollections of placing my faith in God are associated with a promise. Mrs. White, the Good News Club teacher, holds up a tiny leather book with colored pages but no words. As she turns the pages, she explains the way of eternal life and promises us our own Wordless Book if we memorize the verses each page represents. My childish imagination is captivated. And so it was that I first learned about the love of God. Along with the tiny prize, I received Christ as my Savior. Young as I was, it was true faith.

My parents were blue-collar Protestants who seldom attended church. They had six children, twice as many problems, and never enough money. Hardworking and proud, they always tried to manage on their own. I seldom saw them turn to God. During my high school years my father was seriously injured. Unable to cope with the resulting long-term unemployment, he developed a serious drinking problem. As a result our family was thrust into a time of protracted and painful insecurity. This time of instability was used by God to temper and strengthen my faith. I learned that God was a good God who keeps his promises even when life is difficult.

No, Kent did *not* marry a spiritual dependent! My faith pulsated with life and love for the God we both felt called to serve.

But in my present sheltered atmosphere, surrounded by good church people who seldom challenged my faith, was I getting spiritually soft? Was I becoming like the conductor at the train station who has never gone beyond the boundaries of his own city, but imagines he has traveled far because he is always calling out destinations for others? Was I piggybacking on my husband's spiritual journey?

I suddenly felt a chill. "Hang on to my faith," I had said. And now the real question was: Did I have faith for both of us? Was my faith now as strong as it had once been?

But God had prepared me for this. During the months I had observed my husband's inner struggle, I had become increasingly dependent upon the Lord. And with this reliance had come a pervasive sense of well-being. God was with me. And the conscious refrain of my lips and my mind had been "God is good."

Reflecting on the angry thoughts Kent had expressed, I wavered. As I sat in my brightly decorated kitchen, surrounded by yellow gingham and blue chintz, my spirit grew dark. I began to feel some of Kent's despair. Maybe we had believed a lie. Perhaps I was self-deluded. Maybe I should have encouraged him to quit the ministry and cast off whatever it was that was destroying our faith in God.

I felt alone and afraid. I needed reassurance. So I did what I have always done when confronted with fear. I picked up my Bible. My fingers trembled as they traced its gilded edges.

"O God," I cried, "help me."

C. S. Lewis once said that God whispers to us in our joys, speaks to us in our difficulties, and shouts in our pain. I needed his shout.

"Please, Lord, give me a word of encouragement right now."

Though I've never been one to play Bible roulette (and do not recommend it), I took a deep breath and slowly, tremulously opened my old King James Bible. My eye fell on a verse underlined in red. As long as I live I will never forget the soaring, dancing excitement that swept over me as I read eighteen simple words. "Though he fall, he shall not be utterly cast down: for the Lord upholdeth him with his hand" (Psalm 37:24). God didn't shout—he leaped off the pages!

I was spellbound, actually feeling that if I peeked over my shoulder I might see God. I looked at my Bible again and read the line just before the one underlined: "The steps of a good man are ordered by the Lord: and he delighteth in his way." God's presence was so utterly palpable I thought that if I reached out I might touch him. Instead, his everlasting arms reached out and enveloped me.

The oppression was gone and with it, the doubts. God's presence was accompanied by the exhilarating awareness that he indeed did absolutely love and care about us. And with that assurance came tears. "Yes, Kent," I wept, "hang on to my faith."

No one will ever convince me that reading that particular verse at that moment in time was mere coincidence. I know the transcendent God visited *me* right where I was. It was all I needed. With that I joined Kent in bed and fell asleep reciting the promise: "Though he fall, he shall not be utterly cast down: for the Lord upholdeth him with his hand."

The next few days found Kent fluctuating between relief and uncertainty. Glad that he had finally put words to the dark, unsettling thoughts that had grown within him, Kent still battled unanswered questions. While I did not know the answers, I was confident they were to be found.

Later that week I attended a denominational women's meeting where I encountered two friends whose husbands had recently left the ministry. They were together, and what a stunning pair they made. Their studied California chic exuded prosperity—as it was meant to do. *We are doing g-r-r-r-reat!* I could almost hear them purr. In the course of conversation I asked about their spouses, and one replied, "He's never been happier. He's selling life insurance now." She added, "It takes a special kind of man to be in the ministry. You just can't measure your success. And every man must be able to do that in order to have a good self-image."

My mind raced! She echoed my husband's present struggle. Yet I knew there was something terribly wrong with her thinking.

"I've never thought of Kent as extraordinary," I responded, "just called."

"Well," she said with a slight tremor in her voice, "if your church doesn't grow" (and I knew *exactly* what she meant by that—she meant grow *big)*, "Kent is going to feel like a failure."

With that, I became angry, though not at my acquaintance. I was angry that her husband—who at one time felt the call of God to preach the gospel—was now selling insurance. I was angry that the same dark force was presently working on my husband.

I decided I wasn't going to allow it.

"I don't know why," I said with surprising energy, "but you are wrong, and I'm not going to rest until I find out why!"

At home that night I related my conversation to Kent, and our spiritual adrenaline began to flow. The problem had a global dimension. Many people were being affected. We thought of our seminary friends, couples who had said yes to the call of God—and were presently discouraged in ministry. Some were quitting.

The problem was "success." That was what we had to think through. It was a subject we had never attempted to define—not specifically.

I found the tablet on which I had earlier recorded Kent's thoughts and wrote three questions that we considered key:

- Can a man be a success in the ministry and pastor a small church?
- What is failure in the ministry?
- What is success in the ministry?

The two of us sat staring at our list. Expressed in black and white the questions suddenly seemed so cold and crass. What in the world had brought us to ask such questions?

Barbara and I spent considerable time together reflecting on what had brought me to such despair. We replayed the many voices from our past—college chums, church friends, social acquaintances—that had offered advice in some form or other. None of the input was bad in itself, but the underlying premise of the advice, in aggregate, was deadly. Barbara and I summarized the thrust of this counsel:

Marketing. When the church first began, my denomination sent me to an institute for church growth. There I was taught the pragmatic foundations of numerical growth. Very high on the list of essentials was the marketing principle of *visibility and accessibility.* Simply stated, it is this: if you want to sell hamburgers you must make sure that your store is visible to the community and easily accessible. The great hamburger chains live and die by this rule. Smart preachers will do the same. And their churches will grow.

Sociology. In the early stages of planning our church, the church growth expert emphasized that my wife and I must be the right match for the community. He perused the area, met with us observing how we dressed, and asked what our tastes were in such things as clothing, furniture, and education. After analyzing our answers, he pronounced us "perfect" for the work.

The idea, of course, was the "homogenous unit principle." Likes attract and win likes: doctors best evangelize doctors; mechanics, mechanics; athletes, athletes. Our family was just right to lead a growing church in our community.

Stewardship. In the back of my mind I believed that "a church that gives grows" and "a church that gives to missions will be a growing missions church." Giving meant growth. (Thus, I retained a hybrid strain of the prosperity gospel in my unarticulated thinking.) Giving meant getting more people—numerical growth.

Godliness. Also unspoken but firmly rooted in my thinking was the belief that if our people were truly godly and thus exhibiting the fruits of the Spirit, their spiritual ethos would attract both the lost and the searching. Our church would grow.

Certainly no one could question the means. Godliness is a rare quality. Moreover, the growth that would come through authentic Christianity would be eminently healthy. But again, behind this lay the ever-so-subtle thought that godliness was merely a means to something more important, and in this case it was increasing numbers and success.

Preaching. The seminary from which I graduated emphasized the expositional preaching of God's Word. It is an emphasis for which I am grateful. However, though it was never crassly stated, the implicit belief was that if you preach the Word effectively, your church will grow. During my seminary years this belief was unwittingly emphasized by the parade of pulpit stars from large churches brought before us in our daily chapels. My interpretation of this was: growing churches have fine communicators. Those not growing have otherwise.

So the messages kept coming to me, "If you will do this one thing well, your church will grow."

I realized I had been proud of the discriminating use I had made of these principles. I thought that God was going to bless the ministry with great numerical growth because I had not bought into wrong methods and was doing things "right."

But what I did not realize is that while rejecting wrong methods I had bought into the idea that success meant increased numbers. To me success in the ministry meant growth in attendance. Ultimate success meant a big, growing church.

Certainly there is nothing wrong with the wise use of any of the above principles. They should be part of the intelligent orchestration of ministry. However, when the refrain they play is numerical growth—when the persistent motif is numbers—then the siren song becomes deeply sinister: growth in numbers, growth in giving, growth in staff, growth in programs—numbers, numbers, numbers! *Pragmatism* becomes the conductor. The audience inexorably becomes man rather than God. Subtle self-promotion becomes the driving force.

When success in the ministry becomes the same as success in the world, the servant of God evaluates his success like a businessman or an athlete or a politician.

Given my thinking, the only conclusion that I could come to was that I was failing. Knowing what makes a church grow and having done my very best, but having little to show for it, meant I just didn't have it. So the logic went: God had called me to do something for which he had not given me the gifts to succeed. Thus, all my bitter resentment and recriminations.

Years earlier when I began the ministry my motivation was simply to serve Christ. That was all. My heroes were people like Jim Elliot, whose motto—"He is no fool who gives what he cannot keep to gain what he cannot lose"— was part of my life. All I wanted was the approval of God.

But imperceptibly my high Christian idealism had shifted from serving to receiving, from giving to getting. I realized that what I really wanted was a growing church and "success" more than the smile of God.

Subconsciously I was evaluating nearly everything from the perspective of how it would affect church growth. I realized that in the extreme such thinking reduces people to so much "beef on the hoof"—a terrible thought. It also enthrones a relentless pragmatism in church planning. And if this happens, it can erode the noblest ideals. It can even corrupt one's theology.

I realized that I had been subtly seduced by the secular thinking that places a number on everything. Instead of evaluating myself and the ministry from God's point of view, I was using the world's standard of quantitative analysis.

Barbara and I saw the problem exactly. It was like standing at the foot of a great mountain that had to be climbed. The climb would not be easy, but at least we knew what was before us.

So it was in our yellow and blue kitchen, seeming so

much brighter now than in the previous few weeks, that my wife and I bowed in prayer. Each of us prayed earnestly, asking for God's forgiveness and freshly committing ourselves to his service. We asked God to protect us from our cunning adversary who had so subtly seduced us.

We made a covenant to search the Scriptures and learn what God had to say about success. We fiercely determined to evaluate our success from a biblical point of view.

The following chapters describe our journey. What we learned was our liberation from the success syndrome.

It can be yours too!

PART TWO

DEFINITIONS

THREE

Success Is Faithfulness

As Barbara and I searched the Scriptures, we found no place where it says that God's servants are called to be *successful*. Rather, we discovered our call is to be *faithful*.

"So then, men ought to regard us as servants of Christ and as those entrusted with the secret things of God. Now it is required that those who have been given a trust must prove faithful" (1 Corinthians 4:1-2). It is imperative that we fully understand this principle and take it to heart if we are to escape the seductive clutches of the success syndrome.

A vignette from the life of Moses clarified our thinking. Forty years after the dramatic incident at Rephidim where God ordered Moses to strike the rock providing the parched Israelites with water, Moses again faced a thirsty people.

Bitter accusations were hurled at Moses: "If only we had died when our brothers fell dead before the Lord! Why did you bring the Lord's community into this desert, that we and our livestock should die here?" (Numbers 20:3-4). Distraught, Moses and Aaron fell on their faces before God, and God gave them these instructions. "Gather the assembly together. Speak to that rock before their eyes and it will pour out its water." So Moses gathered all Israel around him.

As he surveyed the vast multitude of gripers, his anger

blazed. "'Listen, you rebels, must we bring you water out of this rock?' Then Moses raised his arm and struck the rock twice with his staff. Water gushed out, and the community and their livestock drank." Again, another stupendous miracle! Cool, clear artesian water gushed forth, and every one of the million-plus people and animals drank their fill. This was no streamlet; it was a coursing river.

What a huge success! Moses and Aaron no doubt embraced one another and a thunderous roar rolled across the multitude from horizon to horizon. Moses was again the hero. Through him God met the needs of the people. Israel was miraculously preserved and refreshed. And they gave glory where it belonged—to God. It was another resounding success of Moses' great life.

But that was earth's point of view. From heaven's perspective Moses had sadly failed. In his fury Moses had disregarded God's direction to *speak* to the rock, and instead had struck it twice. His tragic failure was of such proportion he would not fulfill his life's cherished dream of leading Israel into the Promised Land. God said, "Because you did not trust in me enough to honor me as holy in the sight of the Israelites, you will not bring this community into the land I give them."

This tremendous lesson from the life of Moses teaches us that one can be regarded as hugely successful in the ministry and yet be a failure. It is possible to give people *exactly* what they need—the practical exposition of God's Word, inspiring worship, programs that wonderfully meet human needs—and yet be a failure. It is possible to be held up as a paragon of success and to receive the ardent accolades of one's people and be a failure.

The reason Moses so miserably failed was that he was not faithful to God's word. God's primary call is to faithfulness. "It is required that those who have been given a trust must prove faithful" (1 Corinthians 4:2).

Having this foundational principle firmly fixed in our thinking by Moses' tragic experience, Barbara and I were greatly encouraged. Faithfulness, we learned, is possible for all believers, regardless of the size of a person's ministry.

The Obedience Factor

As we further meditated on this we were able to discern two essential elements of faithfulness.

In evaluating success, we must all understand that Scripture consistently links success to obedience—our obedience to God's Word. Following the death of Moses, we find God reiterating this truth to Moses' successor, Joshua, repeating it twice for emphasis, "Be strong and very courageous. Be careful to obey all the law my servant Moses gave you; do not turn from it to the right or to the left, that you may be *successful* wherever you go. Do not let this Book of the Law depart from your mouth; meditate on it day and night, so that you may be careful to do everything written in it. Then you will be prosperous and *successful*" (Joshua 1:7-8, italics mine).[1]

Charles Colson wrote in Prison Fellowship's monthly newsletter, *Jubilee:*

> By the time you read this, we will have dedicated our new national offices near Washington, D.C. As a result of this and other recent expansions, many people have written me to the effect that "God is obviously blessing Prison Fellowship's ministry."
>
> As much as I am sincerely certain that God is, indeed, blessing us, I believe even more certainly that it's a dangerous and misguided policy to measure God's blessing by standards of visible, tangible, material "success."
>
> The inference is that when things are prospering "God is blessing us" and, conversely, that when things are going poorly, or unpublicized, God's blessing is not upon the work or it is unimportant. . . . We must continuously use the measure of our obedience to the

guidelines of his Word as the real—and only—standard of our "success," not some more supposedly tangible or glamorous scale.

With prophetic clarity, Mr. Colson echoes the advice of Scripture and affirms that obedience (*knowing* and explicitly *doing* God's Word) is the key to true success.

The Necessity of Knowing God's Word
It follows that those of us who minister, if we are ever to know true success, must therefore steep ourselves in what the Scriptures call us to do.

A moving incident from the life of John Broadus, one-time president of the University of Virginia and a founding professor at Southern Baptist Seminary, underscores the importance of knowing God's Word. Just three weeks before his death, Broadus stood before his class. The Scripture reading was Acts 18:24: "Now a certain Jew named Apollos, an Alexandrian by birth, an eloquent man, came to Ephesus and he was mighty in the Scriptures." After Broadus read this verse, he went on to say, "Gentlemen, we must be like Apollos, mighty in the Scriptures." A student later said that a hush fell upon that class for the next few minutes as Broadus stood and repeated, "Mighty in the Scriptures . . . mighty in the Scriptures . . . mighty in the Scriptures."[2] That is how we ought to be! As Spurgeon once said, our very blood ought to be "Bibline." This is where success begins and is sustained.

Thus, the question that those of us who desire to succeed in God's service must answer is: Do we know God's Word, and are we growing in our knowledge of it? This is often an embarrassing question, even to the seminary-trained pastors, because advanced theological degrees do not guarantee biblical knowledge. Indeed, we have known seminary graduates who have never *once* read the Bible through! At best, theological education can acquaint us with the language, the nuances of theology, the general arguments of the books, and pastoral methodology. But it cannot insure that we actually know our Bible.

Knowledge of the Bible begins with and is fed by reading God's Word. Every servant must be reading the Scriptures daily, preferably going through the Bible at least once a year. Many of God's most-used servants have made such reading and meditation a part of their lives. We have known some who have read the Bible through a hundred times—one a hundred and fifty times! It is said that George Mueller read the Bible two hundred times. David Livingston read it four times in succession while he was detained in a jungle town.[3] He lived out Spurgeon's dictum: "A Bible which is falling apart usually belongs to someone who is not." William Evans, who in the early part of this century pastored College Church in Wheaton where we now serve, had memorized the entire Bible in the King James and the New Testament in the American Standard Version.[4] Billy Graham says that his medical missionary father-in-law, Nelson Bell, made it a point "to rise every morning at four-thirty and spend two to three hours in Bible reading. He didn't use that time to read commentaries or write; he didn't do his correspondence or any of his other work. He just read the Scriptures every morning, and he was a walking Bible encyclopedia. People wondered at the holiness and the greatness in his life."[5]

Christian co-workers, the call from both the Scriptures and the lives of the faithful is to be people of the Book—to know it and correctly interpret it. If you're not presently engaged in systematic study, why not covenant to, at the very least, read the Scriptures through this year, and put your life in the way of true success?

Knowing and Doing Are Two Different Things
Of course, knowing God's Word isn't enough. Success only comes when his Word is faithfully obeyed. So the

other question we must ask ourselves is: Are we living lives that are obedient to the Scripture? The question is a valid one for us all because, while professing to obey God's Word, we inherently possess an amazing capacity to do otherwise.

Some of us compartmentalize our lives. We imagine that obedience to God's Word in one area means we have obeyed in other areas. Others of us rationalize. For example, one common rationalization is the "many-interpretation" theory—that Scripture is subject to so many interpretations we cannot really know what it means. This is especially convenient when we do not like what it says! But, the fact is God's Word is generally clear. Usually, it's *painfully* clear. As Mark Twain once said, "It's not what I don't understand about the Bible that bothers me; it's what I do understand!"

Success, then, comes when we faithfully study God's Word and faithfully obey it, applying what we understand to all areas of our lives under the direction of the Holy Spirit. A growing knowledge of the Bible matched by a growing obedience is the path to faithfulness and success.

The Glory of What We're Meant to Be

Elisabeth Elliot once stayed in the farmhouse of a Welsh shepherd and his family high in the mountains of North Wales. She stood watching one misty summer morning as the shepherd on horseback herded the sheep with the aid of his champion Scottish collie. The collie, she realized, was in its glory. It was doing what it had been bred and trained to do. Its eyes were always on the sheep, but its ears were delicately tuned to obey its master.

Through obedience the dog experienced its glory. The same is true in the spiritual realm, as Mrs. Elliot insightfully summarized: "To experience the glory of God's will for us means absolute trust. It means the will to do his will, and it means joy."[6] How perfectly right she is! Never are we greater, never do we know greater joy, never are we more successful than when we are obedient to his will.

Such glory, such joy, such success is not just within the range of a selected few, but in reach of us all regardless of our situation. How encouraging this is! Success first begins with obedience to God's Word.

The Hard Work Factor

Some time ago Barbara and I spent a fascinating evening with a young pastor and his wife who had recently begun work in their first pastorate. After dinner we discussed how faithfulness not only demands obedience to God's Word, but hard work.

We thought little of it, until several weeks later when we received the following letter. Our pastor friend wrote:

I feel compelled to make the following comments. Most of what I say is to both my surprise and chagrin.

It seems that in trying to correct some possible pastoral abuses of the past, seminaries are exposing their students to a recurring theme: don't burn out . . . be sure to get your day(s) off . . . marriage first, ministry second." These refrains may all be quite true, but they come with such repetitive force that I fear that the pendulum has swung from those who jeopardized their families in the name of "ministry" to men who think that they have something coming to them because they are "in the ministry." We now have men who are so thoroughly warned of sacrificing their families that they sacrifice nothing!

I say this from my own experience. After my first six months of ministry I was shocked to discover that my biggest danger was not burn out but rusting out. I was lazy! I assumed that I was putting in my forty-plus hours of the ministry, being careful to guard my "time off." But, when I added up my hours I was short of forty. How could this be true of "hardworking Jonathan?"

Fortunately it is not now true of "hardworking Jonathan." His letter was a *de facto* testimony to his handling of the problem.

But his letter does point to a real, ongoing problem with many in the ministry. No one keeps track of a pastor's time. There are no clocks to punch or time cards to turn in. So if a man is not a self-starter, it is so easy to come in late and go home early. It is also very easy to let prayer and sermon preparation slip, and, generally, to imagine that extraneous interests are "ministry." There is more sloth in the pastoral ministry than we like to admit.

But whatever our situation, whether we work too little or too much, we must all agree that there is no such thing as a lazy-faithful servant! That is the point of the Parable of the Talents in Matthew 25:14-20. The slave who was given the five talents multiplied his, as did the slave who was given the two talents. And to each the Lord gave his commendation, "Well done, good and *faithful* slave." But to the slave who did nothing with his talent, the Lord pronounced this withering epithet, "You wicked, *lazy* slave." The Lord has nothing good to say about lazy servants; they are unfaithful.

Jesus himself modeled the energy that he expects from his faithful servants. The Gospel of John tells how Jesus, weary from his ministry and travels, sent his disciples away to get some groceries and sat down to rest. However, as he was "sitting thus" in weary repose by the well, he heard the footfall of an approaching Samaritan woman—another needy soul. In his exhaustion it would have been so easy for him to mutter, "I've been ministering to thousands. I've got to have time to rest. I'll just keep my eyes shut and ignore her." Not Jesus! He went for her soul in one of the most beautiful displays of gracious aggression in all of Scripture. He continued to minister when necessary, even at the point of exhaustion. And we, if we are faithful, will do as our Master did!

A caveat is in order here. Scripture does not call us to

obsessive-compulsive workaholism. God's Word fully recognizes the humanity of his servants—the need to care for the body and give it proper rest and relaxation. But the fact remains that a faithful servant will be hardworking, and when necessary, labor on in exhaustion. The Apostle Paul told the Corinthians, "I have labored and toiled and have often gone without sleep; I have known hunger and thirst and have often gone without food; I have been cold and naked. Besides everything else, I face daily the pressure of my concern for all the churches. Who is weak, and I do not feel weak? Who is led into sin, and I do not inwardly burn?" (2 Corinthians 11:27-29).

It was a banner day in our lives when we saw from the Bible that great public success in the ministry, like that of Moses at Kadesh, is not necessarily success in God's eyes. *God's call is to be faithful rather than successful.*

This brought Barbara and me to a profound and liberating realization. We saw how success was equally possible for those in the most difficult of situations—for example, those with small numbers and inadequate resources—as well as those having vast ministries.

We were under no illusions about faithfulness being easy in our situation, but we could see that it was possible for us by God's grace. The essential elements of faithfulness are within reach of us all. How encouraging!

Fellow servants, we all go through difficult times. They are the baggage of any ministry. Times of immense joy will be matched by times of criticism, times of doubt, and even times of sorrow.

When these come, delve deep into God's Word. Read it and reread it. Meditate over it upon your knees. Recommit yourself to letting his Word "richly dwell within you." Then, as it speaks to you, faithfully obey it with all your might, and keep on working hard for God. In doing this your life will be further grounded in faithfulness *and* success, for a faithful life is a successful life.

FOUR

Success Is Serving

In 1878, when William Booth's Salvation Army was beginning to make its mark, men and women from all over the world began to enlist. One man, who had once dreamed of becoming a bishop, crossed the Atlantic from America to England to enlist. Samuel Brengle left a fine pastorate to join Booth's Army. But at first General Booth accepted his services reluctantly and grudgingly. Booth said to Brengle, "You've been your own boss too long." And in order to instill humility in Brengle, he set him to work cleaning the boots of other trainees. Discouraged, Brengle said to himself, "Have I followed my own fancy across the Atlantic in order to black boots?" And then, as in a vision, he saw Jesus bending over the feet of rough, unlettered fishermen. "Lord," he whispered, "you washed their feet; I will black their shoes."[1]

As Samuel Logan Brengle willingly and lovingly bent over those dirty boots, he experienced servanthood and therefore *success*, for he was living like Jesus. Evidently, it was a lesson well learned: Brengle went on to live a life of profound servanthood, even as the Army's first American-born commissioner.

Samuel Brengle's example provides an inspiring model for us all. But quite frankly, inspiring as Brengle's life is, such a life does not come easily to most believers. In fact, even the apostles had difficulty with servanthood.

Matthew reports that toward the end of Jesus' ministry an ugly, competitive spirit developed among the apostles when James and John and their mother attempted to get Jesus to promise privileged thrones in the kingdom. Matthew says, "When the ten heard about this, they were indignant with the two brothers" (Matthew 20:24). Harsh words and angry gestures were exchanged among the twelve. Tempers flared! So Jesus called them together and said: "You know that the rulers of the Gentiles lord it over them, and their high officials exercise authority over them. Not so with you. Instead, whoever wants to become great among you must be your servant, and whoever wants to be first must be your slave—just as the Son of Man did not come to be served, but to serve, and to give his life as a ransom for many" (Matthew 20:25-28).

It would seem that none could miss the point. However, as we all know, hearing the truth and making it part of our lives are not the same thing, even when we are devoted to Christ. Several days later, when the apostles arrived in Jerusalem to celebrate the Passover, they were still going at it.

Peter and John had secured a room for Passover as Jesus had directed, but they had neglected to make arrangements for foot-washing. And as the apostles wandered in, no one would condescend to perform the humble task. Jesus' teaching, as direct as it was, had apparently had no effect. No one would volunteer for the lowly task. How very human they were. How very human we are.

The conductor of a great symphony orchestra was once asked which was the most difficult instrument to play. "The second violin," he answered. "I can get plenty of first violinists, but to find someone who can play second violin with enthusiasm—that is a problem. And if we have no second violin, we have no harmony."

At that tragic moment among the apostles, there were no "second fiddles." And certainly no harmony. They desperately needed to be taught—and taught well.

An Astonishing Example
As John's Gospel continues the account, the disciples are reclining at the table with their shamefully dirty feet stretching out behind them. The meal is in process, but the conversation is strained because of the tension. What a miserable way to eat Passover! Soon they become aware that the Teacher has risen from supper and is standing apart from them.

> As they watched he removed his outer garment and then his tunic. He was completely disrobed, naked.
> Next, he took a towel and wrapped it about his body.
> And then he poured water into a basin, and began slowly to move about the circle, washing each of the disciples' outstretched feet, wiping them with the towel with which he was wrapped.[2]

It was an electrifying act. The Midrash taught that no Hebrew, even a slave, could be commanded to wash feet.[3] Yet, Jesus did it in the most humble way possible, clothed only in a servant's towel. In the breathless silence of that upper room, the apostles heard the trickle of water as it was poured, the friction of the towel as their feet were wiped off, the sound of the Master breathing as he moved from one to another. What we wouldn't give to see the astonishment on their faces! The Incarnate Son, God himself, had stripped himself naked and *washed the feet* of his prideful, arrogant creatures.

Then he said, "Now that I, your Lord and Teacher, have washed your feet, you also should wash one another's feet. I have set you an example that you should do as I have done for you. I tell you the truth, no servant is greater than his master, nor is a messenger greater than the one who sent him" (John 13:14-16).

Jesus used the ancient logic: If it is true for the greater (me) then it must be true for the lesser (you). It is always a powerful argument. But coming from his infinitude, it is infinitely compelling! If the God of the universe is a servant, how dare we, his creatures, be anything else?

The "It's Hard to Find Good Help These Days" Syndrome

Today, service and sacrifice are definitely not in vogue. The "great" ones of this world straddle thrones and give orders. They measure their power by how many people they command. They do not serve; they are served. The great ones live out the antithesis of Christ's example.

To be honest, this is also true for much of the church. There is a mindset—who knows where it comes from?— that defines success as a kind of lordship: sitting in the honored seat, being the feted guest at luncheons, speaking to vast throngs, building monuments, collecting honorary titles, etc. Whatever you call it, it's a philosophy that values the business of being served.

We well remember attending a ministers' retreat in which the featured speaker, himself a minister, told us that if we had extravagant desires for material possessions, then it was God's will for us to have our desires fulfilled. His reasoning? Psalm 37:4: "Delight yourself in the Lord and he will give you the desires of your heart." Thus, we were told that if we were delighting in the Lord, and yet had a desire for a Cadillac (like the speaker's) it was God's will! "After all, the King's servants travel first class." Never mind the faulty exegesis! Never mind the unbiblical, simplistic deductions about the desires of the regenerate! Never mind that the symbol of Christianity is the cross!

> Name it and claim it, that's what faith's about!
> You can have what you want if you just have no doubt.
> So make out your "wish list" and keep on believin'
> And you will find yourself perpetually receivin'.[4]

For those caught up in such thinking, Christianity exists to give *me* eternal life, to increase *my* physical health, to coddle *my* body, to enlarge *my* power, to elevate *my* prestige, and give *me* money for whatever *my* heart desires.

Is it really possible for a minister of the gospel to live this way? Of course! Read your Bible: the disciples were heading for the same Cadillac dealership. Read church history. Read about the current church scandals in the newspaper. Read your own heart, and listen to the words of poet Robert Raines:

> *I am like James and John*
> *Lord, I size up other people*
> > *in terms of what they can do for me;*
> > *how they can further my program,*
> > > *feed my ego,*
> > > *satisfy my needs,*
> > > *give me strategic advantage.*
>
> *I exploit people,*
> > > *ostensibly for your sake,*
> > > *but really for my own sake.*
>
> *Lord, I turn to you*
> > *to get the inside track*
> > *and obtain special favors,*
> > > *your direction for my schemes,*
> > > *your power for my projects,*
> > > *your sanction for my ambitions,*
> > > *your blank checks for whatever I want.*
>
> *I am like James and John.* [5]

The current that pulls us from service to self-service is subtle and often imperceptible. Such a gradual undertow, of course, also tugs us from success to failure. We must be aware of this danger and quiz ourselves: Were we once serving God, and now serving self? Are we in the process of making such a change, just drifting with the current? How can we recommit ourselves to ministries of servant-hood, following the example of Christ?

The Story Inside the Story

Perhaps in retrospect the disciples could see, just as we can, that in the ritual of foot-washing Christ portrayed his entire life of servanthood, from his incarnation to his earthly ministry to his death to his ascension:

- *He "rose from supper."* Just as in the incarnation, he rose from the place of fellowship with God the Father and the Holy Spirit.
- *He "laid aside His garments."* Throughout his ministry on earth, Christ temporarily set aside his glorious existence. "Who, being in very nature God, did not consider equality with God something to be grasped, but made himself nothing" (Philippians 2:6-7).
- *"He poured water into the basin, and began to wash the disciples' feet, and to wipe them with the towel with which He was girded."* Likewise, Christ poured out his blood on the cross to wash away the sins of guilty mankind (Philippians 2:8).
- *"When He had washed their feet, and taken His garments, and reclined at table again. . . ."* "After he had provided purification for sins, he sat down at the right hand of the Majesty in heaven" (Hebrews 1:3).

The Cross as the Ultimate Symbol of Success

Everything about Jesus' life shouts service! And the ultimate expression of his servanthood was the cross. There, hanging on the cross, was the Servant *par excellence*, performing the ultimate service.

Wherever we may be on the path of servanthood, there is one thing we all must do if we are to be servants, and that is look to the cross. It is the crowning event of Christ's servant life, just as Jesus had said: "The Son of Man did not come to be served, but to serve, and to give his life as a ransom for many" (Matthew 20:28; Mark 10:45).

So here's one secret of successful ministry: When we keep our eyes upon the cross, we want to serve. Friends and co-workers, if we have been chafing under our ministerial burdens, possibly wondering if we have followed our own fancies, we need to envision Christ washing the feet of rough, unlettered fishermen. We need to see Christ on the cross washing our sins away as the Ultimate Servant. And then we need to whisper, "Lord, you washed their feet; you washed away my sins. I will serve you and your church. Amen."

Serving God through Preaching, Administrating, and Counseling

Three forms of service are central to many people's ministries and deserve further mention in the context of servanthood:

Preaching. Paul's words, "So then, men ought to regard us as servants of Christ and as those entrusted with the secret things of God" (1 Corinthians 4:1), tell us that a primary avenue of servanthood is preaching the truths of the gospel.

Preaching, because it is an authoritative function, may not seem to be service. But properly understood, it is. The faithful steward of God's mysteries must spend long hours of unseen labor to acceptably preach the Word (2 Timothy 2:15). Moreover, the proper demeanor in the pulpit is that of a servant with a message from the Master that must faithfully be proclaimed (2 Corinthians 4:5). Faithfulness in the pulpit requires a vast investment of time and energy and is a great service to Christ and his church, whether recognized by the church or not. Those who would honor God in the pulpit must be servants.

Administering. The quality of leadership necessarily demands that servants be administrators, "helmsmen of the church," who direct its life and action (1 Corinthians 12:28). We might define administration as "ruling through humble service." Some in the ministry gladly embrace administrative duties, truly enjoying the calls, dictation, meetings, and many tedious tasks necessary to good administration. Others experience revulsion toward it, feeling they would rather do anything else. Whatever one's natural reaction to executive duties, the proper attitude for the pastor is that of a humble servant. Do we see our executive duties as opportunities to serve Christ? If we do, we will be encouraged to give our very best to him in loving, efficient administration.

Counseling. Paul charges us, "Carry each other's burdens, and in this way you will fulfill the law of Christ" (Galatians 6:2). Here the pastoral ministry provides vast opportunity for servanthood because we are very often the ones to whom people turn to unburden themselves. When hurting people come to us, we first serve them by truly listening and sometimes even weeping with them. This, in itself, is a singular act of love in an uncaring world. We also bear their burdens by offering the wise counsel of God's Word and enlisting the help of others in the church as is appropriate. Finally, we bear their burdens by making them part of our regular prayers. Thus pastoral counseling compels us to serve others much in the way the Lord would if he were still here on earth.

Fellow servants, the common ministerial functions of preaching, administering, and counseling are just a few of the privileged ways that the ministry provides to serve and to develop a Christlike life.

Servanthood, as we have seen, yields success—because in serving we become more like Christ. Here Barbara and I observed one of the privileged benefits of the ministry: by providing so many ways to serve, one continually experiences the side-effect of developing a more Christlike life.

Seeing this afresh, Barbara and I thanked God that we were not following our fancies but rather a divine call that provides many opportunities for success. We had discovered that in service—not self-service—is the true pursuit of success!

FIVE

Success Is Loving

A number of years ago a fascinating interview took place between Mr. Charles Schwab, then president of Bethlehem Steel, and Ivy Lee, a self-styled management consultant. Lee was an aggressive, self-confident man who by his perseverance had secured the interview with Mr. Schwab, who was no less self-assured, being one of the most powerful men in the world. During the conversation, Mr. Lee asserted that if the management of Bethlehem Steel would follow his advice, the company's operations would be improved and their profits increased.

Schwab responded, "If you can show us a way to get more things done, I'll be glad to listen; and if it works, I'll pay you whatever you ask within reason."

Lee handed Schwab a blank piece of paper and said, "Write down the most important things you have to do tomorrow."

Mr. Schwab did so.

"Now," Lee continued, "number them in order of importance."

Schwab did so.

"Tomorrow morning start on number one, and stay with it until you have completed it. Then go on to number two and number three and number four. . . . Don't worry if you haven't completed everything by the end of the day. At least you will have completed the most important projects. Do this every day. After you have been convinced of the value of this system, have your men try it. Try it as long as you like, and then send me your check for whatever you think the advice is worth."

The two men shook hands and Lee left the president's office. A few weeks later Charles Schwab sent Ivy Lee a check for $25,000—an astronomical amount in the 1930s! He said it was the most profitable lesson he had learned in his long business career.

In the cold, hard business world there are few things more important to success than learning how to set priorities and live by them. It is no less important in the spiritual life, where we must have our priorities in order if we hope to experience success. And in the spiritual realm the number one priority is loving God.

Loving God

Nowhere is this more fully dramatized than in our Lord's dealings with Peter in John 21, the great final chapter of John's Gospel. As the curtain lifts on this final episode, the backdrop is the early morning Sea of Tiberias, the stage is a rocky beach set with a glowing fire, and the *dramatis personae* are Jesus Christ, Peter, and six other disciples seated about the fire. Everything is in place for an immortal exchange between Peter and the Risen Christ, which will clarify the importance of love for all time.

To understand fully what will be said about the priority of love, we must appreciate the massive sense of failure that gripped Peter's soul. Peter was the recent owner of the world's most infamous denial. It was just two weeks before, on the eve of the crucifixion, that he denied the Lord three times. The final denial was a sweaty, sordid thing in which, cursing and swearing, he said, "I do not know this man you are talking about!" It was a terrible moment, and in the heat of his denial Peter had not seen his Master emerge from the inner chamber. Jesus had seen it all!

The meeting of their eyes has to be one of the most painful exchanges in human experience, as with the echoes of the cock's crow still ringing in the morning darkness, Jesus' guiltless, unblinking, knowing eyes looked into the heart of Peter. Peter went out into the night and wept bitterly. But those tears could not wash Jesus from his mind. He would never forget.

All of this was firmly lodged in Peter's psyche as he sat before the fire. He had played those tapes a thousand times. Sure the resurrection had taken place, and the Lord had appeared and said, "Peace be with you," but Peter had not yet pulled himself together. His sense of failure was immense.

As the morning mists rose from the lake and the smoke wafted about, a tense silence gripped Peter and the disciples when Christ appeared among them. John reports that "none of the disciples ventured to question him, 'Who are you?' knowing that it was the Lord."

Divine Surgery

How Peter's heart must have jumped as the Lord broke the silence: "Simon, son of John, do you love me more than these?"

There it was, out in the open air. The Lord had really put it to him.

John does not describe for us the way Peter looked as he was jolted by these penetrating words, but from our common experience we can well imagine: Peter's heart raced, his stomach turned, his cheeks burned, and his eyes teared. He felt and looked terrible.

But these words were divinely surgical. Jesus addressed him as *Simon*, which was Peter's name before he met him. The Lord was intentionally avoiding his Lord-given title, Peter—the rock. The salutation was calculated to cut—and that it did, perfectly.

Jesus had also asked Peter if he loved him *more* than the other disciples did. Again Peter's thoughts could not help but flash back to what he had said to the Lord in the upper room: "Even if all fall away on account of you, I never will" (Matthew 26:33). What agony Christ's question must have brought upon Peter!

Then, of course, there was the charcoal fire on the beach—*just like the one in the high priest's courtyard where Peter had denied the Lord.* The aroma of the smoking coals and Jesus' unblinking eyes resurrected in Peter the memory of that terrible moment of failure. Everything the Lord did was divinely calculated, like a surgeon with a scalpel, to reopen Peter's tender wounds. Failure throbbed in him. And the question hung in the air waiting to be answered, "Simon son of John, do you truly love [agape] me more than these?" (John 21:15).

No one moved in the silence. Then Peter softly replied, "Yes, Lord; you know that I have affection for you." Peter could not bring himself to use the Lord's word *agape.* So he substituted *philia*—love, friendship love, deep affection— in his answer. And Jesus answered, "Tend my lambs." In other words, "If you have what you claim, then you may serve."

Taking a Retest

Painful as it was for Peter, Jesus was not finished with his line of questioning. He followed with a second probing question, "Simon, son of John, do you love me?"

Christ was saying, "Simon, dropping all comparison with the others, the simple question is not, 'Do you have affection for me,' but 'Do you *agape* [love] me?' This is the bottom line. Answer me."

Again the only motion around the fire was the drifting smoke. And Peter meekly and carefully answered, "Yes, Lord. You know I have affection for you."

We must understand that Peter's answer was not a bad answer. 1 Corinthians 16:22 says, "If anyone does not [have a friendship] love [for] the Lord—a curse be on him.

Come, O Lord!" Friendship love is a wonderful love and perfectly proper toward God. But poor, failed Peter could not bring himself to use the Savior's word, *agape* love.

Jesus' response was, "Shepherd my sheep."

The Final Question
There is violence in the Lord's questioning, but it is a loving, gracious violence. Jesus is doing something wonderful for Peter.

He said to him the third time, "Simon, son of John, do you love me?" (literally, "Do you have a friendship love for me?"). The Lord has assumed Peter's word, and questions its reality: "Simon," he is saying, "do you really have this affection for me that you have claimed? Do you?"

The three incisions were completed. In the first question the Lord has challenged Peter's rock-likeness and the superiority of his love. In the second he questioned whether he had any love at all. And in the third he challenged Peter's humble claim to a less exalted "affection" love.

Peter's agony peaked. John tells us that Peter was "grieved" (literally *pained*). But out of his pain he lovingly answered, "Lord, you know all things. You know that I [have a friendship] love [for] you." He threw himself on the Lord's perfect knowledge. Peter loved Jesus with the deepest of loves, but his illusions, his presumptions about himself, were stripped away.

And for the Lord, that was enough, and he said in finality, "Tend my sheep."

Peter's restoration was accomplished! And they all saw it. In retrospect they came to see that the Lord had choreographed everything. Originally, there were three questions followed by three denials. Now, over his carefully laid charcoal fire, there were:

Three questions—three confessions—three commissions!

Peter's heart soared in relief.

The Quintessential Question

The consummate drama of Christ and Peter has been preserved for the church to establish once and for all the abiding principle that, *Before all things, even service to God, we must love God with all of our hearts.* It is the highest priority in life! It is the first question for every theologian, every pastor, every missionary. It is the quintessential question for everyone who wants to please God.

The truth is, God has always made the priority clear. From earliest times he was explicit: "Hear, O Israel: The Lord our God, the Lord is one. Love the Lord your God with all your heart and with all your soul and with all your strength" (Deuteronomy 6:4-5).

Everything we have is to be devoted to our loving God. This theme was substantiated and solemnized by the Lord himself when a lawyer asked him, "Teacher, which is the greatest commandment in the Law?" To which Jesus answered, 'You shall love the Lord your God with all your heart and with all your soul and with all your mind. This is the first and greatest commandment" (Matthew 22:37-38). From Jesus' own lips we hear that nothing, nothing is of greater importance!

Love and Service

Barbara and I rediscovered this fundamental truth and were refreshed by the reality that there is no success apart from loving God.

We *re*discovered it because it was, of course, something we already knew but something that had quietly been smothered by ministerial misery. Peter's stunning rapprochement with Christ freshened this truth for us and fixed it like the polestar in our minds. It is now the heart of our souls' navigation.

We were also refreshed by this truth because in bringing clarity to my thinking it affirmed that *prima facie* success, what appears at first glance to be success, is not necessarily success in God's economy.

We began to apply this principle to the ministries that we knew. Immediately four thoughts popped out:

1. It is possible to pastor a huge church and not love God.
2. It is possible to design and preside over perfectly conceived and executed worship services and not love God.
3. It is possible to preach insightful, biblical, Christ-exalting sermons and not love God.
4. It is even possible to write books that deepen others' love for God and not love God.

The truth is, it is more than just possible. For to our great sorrow, it is happening all too often! The unfortunate revelations from the lives of some of our prominent Christian leaders so sadly reveal misplaced priorities. Not only are the high places not safe, but they may be particularly dangerous. Apparently, the high places must be assumed only with the greatest care.

Love Liberates
The realization that loving God is the ground of all true success is truly liberating. How?

First, it places our lives and ministries beyond the fallible, oppressive judgment of the quantifiers—the statistics keepers.

Second, it liberates us from the destructive tendency to compare ourselves with others. After all, who can measure the love of another's heart? Realizing this, we need not feel discouraged or embarrassed by a ministry that may not be outwardly or numerically successful. Our dignity and accomplishment lie in our relationship to God and our love for him.

Third, it frees and motivates us to live our life's highest priority, because if we *really do believe* that loving God is the most important thing in life, then everything—our conversation, our schedules, our ambitions—will progressively reflect his love. There is a sublime, ongoing liberation to love that comes from understanding that the love of God is the most important thing in life.

Finally, it is freeing to the *whole* church, regardless of status, because loving God is something equally open to all. The ability to love him is not determined by stature or standing in the ecclesiastical world. Nor is it tied to ability. University education, intellectual aptitude, and even theological eloquence are no advantage in loving God. Indeed, the process of loving God may even be *hindered* by prominence! The possibility of intensely loving him is equally open to all, from the archbishop to the gardener. Loving God is a sublimely egalitarian call. It is singularly liberating amid our name-dropping, status-conscious world.

Barbara and I experienced a new surge of freedom as we refreshed ourselves to this truth. And we committed ourselves to loving God above all things, regardless of whatever happened in the rest of life. This commitment, we felt, involved three ingredients.

The first ingredient is absolute honesty regarding our love for God. In Peter's final exchange with the Lord over the charcoal fire he said, "Lord, you know all things." The word he used for *know* meant personal, intimate knowledge. In effect, he said, "Lord, you have walked with me. You have watched me personally for years. You know me intimately in every way. I cannot fool you. You know the depth of my love for you." And, indeed, he did know! Likewise, he knows exactly how much each of us loves him.

In light of this, I have developed a helpful spiritual exercise. It is to imagine myself alone on the shore facing Christ as he is silhouetted against the sea of eternity. He is looking at me with his loving, all-knowing eyes and says, "Kent, do you love me? Dropping all comparisons, do you really love me? Do you have affection for me?"

I answer honestly. There is nothing else I can do, because *he knows*. And it is the integrity of my answer that makes my growth in love possible. We must all honestly confess the truth about our love for God before we can be helped.

It is the foundational question. And that is the question we ask you to answer. Do you really love him? Tell him the truth. He already knows. But in telling him, you will be telling yourself the truth. That is where we must all begin.

After honesty, the second ingredient in developing our love for God is to cultivate earnestly the conscious inner ability to love him while we serve him. This is significant because it is too easy to think that service of him presupposes love—like the "devoted husband" who had *not* told his wife he loved her for twenty years. His reasoning? "Twenty years of faithfulness demonstrates my love." But does it? The Bible suggests otherwise, as in the case of the Prodigal Son's older brother, whose seemingly devoted service was actually devoid of love. Fellow workers, we must consciously express our love to God as we wade through administrative red tape, sit through committee meetings, preach a sermon or teach a Bible study, share in the joy of a wedding or the sorrow of a funeral. Only by making our expression of love an integral part of our daily service will our love for him—and our ministry for the kingdom—grow.

The third ingredient necessary for enhancing our love for God is to spend special time with him. Simply stated, we spend time with those whom we love. The more time we spend with God, the more we will love him. We all must discipline ourselves to take special time to love God, to think deep upon his holiness, to love him, to glory in the cross, to say, "Abba Father, dearest Father! I love you! I love you! I love you!"

SIX

Success Is Believing

There is a refrain I can't get out of my head. It is "Believe what you believe." For me it points to one of the great needs of Christians—which is not to believe more and better things, but to believe what we already believe. During my bout with success, my faith had slipped so miserably that I was not believing the things I actually did believe. Illogical, you think? Then follow me in considering the relationship of belief and success.

The writer of Hebrews, in the famous section on faith, makes a straightforward statement regarding the importance of faith: "Without faith it is *impossible* to please God." There it is. There is no way around it. God simply will take no pleasure in our accomplishments, no matter how great they may be, apart from faith. Thus, it can be fairly said that *without faith, there is no success.*

The writer continues: "Without faith it is impossible to please God, because anyone who comes to him must believe that he exists and that he rewards those who earnestly seek him" (Hebrews 11:6). Quite clearly, a faith that is acceptable to God believes two things: (1) it believes that *God exists*, and (2) it believes that *God rewards* his people, that he is positively active on their behalf.[1]

Believing God Exists
Obviously, believing that God exists means that one must believe in the objective reality of God, that he really does

exist. But here in the context of Hebrews, a belief that "God is" means that one must believe that the sovereign miracle-working God of the Old Testament, the God of Scripture, exists.

This the saints of Hebrews 11 believed. They believed that God was all-powerful, all-present, and all-knowing, and that he was holy, just, good, gracious, merciful, and wise—not because they listed his attributes as the later theologians would do—but simply because they believed what their history and prophets and Scripture and experience taught them. They believed that this stupendous God existed.

And, having this belief, they took the major step toward a faith that pleases God, because such a profound belief in God naturally goes on to believe "that he rewards those who earnestly seek him," that he is positively active on the part of his people.

Believing That God Rewards Those Who Seek Him

Those in the Hebrews 11 "Hall of Faith" certainly believed that God would reward them, though often it was difficult to see how.

Some were called to trust in God's ultimate equity while suffering unrelieved unto death. Our text says of them that they "were tortured and refused to be released, so that they might gain a better resurrection." Still others were called upon to believe for specific promises in this life—like Moses who by faith obeyed God and led Israel through the Red Sea.

But whether these great people of faith were called to focus their belief on God's rewards in history or in eternity, they all believed that God was actively working in them and through them and for them, and would reward them even though they could not always see or understand how.

Without this faith, it is impossible to please God. Without this faith, life cannot be called a success—no matter what others may call it.

Believing What We Believe

Part of the problem during those dark days in our ministry was faith: I was not believing what I believed. How was this? To be sure, I was not consciously disbelieving that God is or that he rewards those who seek him. As a matter of fact, I would have fought those who denied these truths. Yet there was a sense in which the reality of the things I believed about God had faded. The massive implications of his existence had been minimized by the inward focus of my anxious heart. The truth that he is the equitable rewarder was suppressed by my miserable preoccupation with my present circumstances. My jeremiad on that dark night of my soul, in which I concluded that I was the butt of a cruel joke and actually said, "God is not good," testifies to my failing belief.

I truly was not believing what I believed! My life was not pleasing to God. And I certainly was not successful—for there can be no success apart from God's smile.

What I needed, and what was to come in the following weeks, was a rebirth of faith, a new believing in what I already believed. To be perfectly candid, it did not come in a neat, organized package; nor did it come all at once, or in a particular order. It came gradually in bits and pieces. Much of it was unconscious, and some of it I was aware of. But, in retrospect, I see that it crystallized in the divine categories of faith as here described in Hebrews:

The God of Scripture exists. For those of us on this side of the cross, the truth to be believed is, as we know, utterly mind-boggling! In addition to the massive truths about God known to the Old Testament saints, we, through the incarnation of Christ, can understand even more. The God of the New Testament is not greater than the God of the Old Testament, but the New Testament revelation of

God is greater. As the Apostle John so beautifully said, "No one has ever seen God, but God the One and Only [Jesus], who is at the Father's side, has made him known" (John 1:18). Jesus explained (literally *exegeted)* God to us! Thus, the potential vastness of our belief is tremendously enlarged.

Paul's great "Hymn of the Incarnation" (Colossians 1:15-18) has done this for me as in it Jesus is revealed as the Creator, Sustainer, and Goal of creation.

Christ the Creator. The hymn sings of his creatorship: "For by him all things were created: things in heaven and on earth, visible and invisible, whether thrones or powers or rulers or authorities; all things were created by him and for him" (Colossians 1:16). He created the invisible spirit world, for that is what "thrones . . . powers . . . rulers . . . authorities" refer to. He also created the vast visible world and universe.

Think of it. He created everything! He created the fires of Arcturus and the firefly. He created the colors of the spectrum—aquamarine, electric blue, orange, saffron, vermilion. He created every texture, every living thing, every planet, every star, every speck of stellar dust in the most forgotten backwash of the universe! And he did it all *ex nihilo,* from nothing. He had no rabbit and no hat!

This is the God that I believed in, that all believers trust. But a spiritual renaissance began in my heart as I further believed what I believed.

Christ the Sustainer. The song goes on to tell of his sustaining power: "He is before all things, and in him all things hold together" (Colossians 1:17). There is a medieval painting that shows Christ in the clouds with the world of humans and nature below. And from Christ to every object is painted a thin golden thread. The artist was portraying this same truth in Colossians—that Christ is responsible for sustaining the existence of every created thing.

The tense used in the Greek emphasizes that he continues *presently* to hold all things together, and thus apart from his continuous action, all would disintegrate.

He is the force, the ultimate unifying force the physicists are searching for, which holds every speck of matter, and, in fact, every incorporeal spirit, together!

Astounding! The pen I write with, the book you hold, your very breath that falls upon this page are all held together by Christ. And if he, for one millisecond, ceased his power, it all would be gone!

We believe this, do we not? But do we actually, existentially, in our heart of hearts, believe it? If we do, then we have a Christology that will see us through the most difficult of times and give birth to even greater faith.

Do we believe that "he is?" Do we *truly* believe what we believe? That is the question.

Christ the Goal. The majestic truths of his creatorship and sustaining power virtually demand this truth. "All things were created . . . for him" (Colossians 1:16). This is an astonishing statement. There is nothing like it anywhere in biblical literature.[2] The sense is even more astonishingly dramatic when "for him" is translated "toward him," as some have done. Thus it reads, "All things have been created by him and toward him."[3] All creation is moving toward its goal in him. Everything began with him and will end with him.

He is the starting point of the universe and its consummation.

All things sprang forth at his command, and all things will return at his command.

He is the beginning and he is the end—both Alpha and Omega.

Everything in creation, history, and spiritual reality is moving toward him and for him!

We believe this. But do we really believe it?

Christ the Loving Head. The Hymn of the Incarnation ends with this thought: "He is the head of the body, the church; he is the beginning and the firstborn from among

the dead, so that in everything he might have the suprem-
acy" (Colossians 1:18). So we conclude that Christ the
head is to be preeminent in all of life. And then follows
the explanation: "For God was pleased to have all his fullness dwell in him, and through him to reconcile to himself
all things, whether things on earth or things in heaven, by
making peace through his blood, shed on the cross" (Colossians 1:19-20).

Our great God, Jesus Christ, reconciled us by his own
blood on the cross! *How* could the Creator, Sustainer, and
Goal of the universe do this? *Why* did he do this? Our
minds become exhausted in contemplation of this, and we
are driven to this explanation, for there can be no other:
"For God so loved the world that he gave his one and only
Son, that whoever believes in him shall not perish but
have eternal life" (John 3:16). The Creator, Sustainer, and
Goal loves us—and the cross is the measure of his love.

> *In the Cross of Christ I glory,*
> *Towering o'er the wrecks of time!*

Christ the Creator, Sustainer, Goal, and Lover of my Soul.
What you believe about Christ is everything. If you believe
that he is *Creator* of everything, every cosmic speck across
trillions of light years of trackless space, the Creator of the
textures and shapes and colors which dazzle our eyes; if
you believe that he is the *Sustainer* of all creation, the force
presently holding the atoms of your body and this universe together, and that without him all would dissolve; if
you believe that he is the *Goal* of everything, that all creation is moving toward him; if you further believe that this
God is the *Lover* of your soul—then you believe in the God
that "is," you believe that the God of the Holy Scriptures
exists!

As believers we do believe this. Anything less is sub-
Christian. But do we *really* believe it? Again, do we truly
believe what we believe? Think about it . . . for if your

belief is deepening, though you have been a believer for years, it will change your life right now.

Why? Because such belief assures you that your life is in the hands of a sovereign God, and not a twig tossed about by the tides of life.

Why else? Because you believe that you are the object of an infinite love, which desires the best for you.

Why else is it life changing? Because, with such a God as this, you have no option but to believe "that he is a rewarder of those who seek him."

As I mentioned earlier, it did not happen all at once, and it was not neat or systematic. Nevertheless, I gradually experienced a revival of belief that "he is," and this inevitably led me and Barbara to the assurance that "he is a rewarder of those who seek him."

My outward lack of "success" did not change. But, I can tell you this: Barbara and I sensed the peace of God that, we believe, came from his smile.

An experience from the life of Ira Sankey dramatically underlines the all-caring God we serve. It was Christmas Eve 1875 and Sankey was traveling on a Delaware River steamboat when he was recognized by some of the passengers. His picture had been in the newspaper because he was the song leader for the famous evangelist D. L. Moody. They asked him to sing one of his own hymns, but Sankey demurred, saying that he preferred to sing William B. Bradbury's hymn "Savior Like a Shepherd Lead Us." As he sang, one of the stanzas began, "We are Thine; do Thou befriend us. Be the Guardian of our way."

When he finished, a man stepped from the shadows and asked, "Did you ever serve in the Union army?"

"Yes," Mr. Sankey answered, "in the spring of 1860."

"Can you remember if you were doing picket duty on a bright, moonlit night in 1862?"

"Yes," Mr. Sankey answered, very much surprised.

"So did I, but I was serving in the Confederate army. When I saw you standing at your post, I thought to myself, 'That fellow will never get away alive.'

"I raised my musket and took aim. I was standing in the shadow, completely concealed, while the full light of the moon was falling upon you. At that instant, just as a moment ago, you raised your eyes to heaven and began to sing. . . .

"'Let him sing his song to the end,' I said to myself, 'I can shoot him afterwards. He's my victim at all events, and my bullet cannot miss him.'

"But the song you sang then was the song you sang just now. I heard the words perfectly: 'We are Thine; do Thou befriend us. Be the Guardian of our way.'

"Those words stirred up many memories. I began to think of my childhood and my God-fearing mother. She had many times sung that song to me.

"When you had finished your song, it was impossible for me to take aim again. I thought, 'The Lord who is able to save that man from certain death must surely be great and mighty.' And my arm of its own accord dropped limp at my side."[4]

How utterly amazing is our God and his keeping power! Such a story along with the supreme truths we have been studying suggest some questions:

1. Am I believing that God can take care of me?
    Answer it truthfully.
2. Am I believing he loves me?
    Again, answer it truthfully.
3. Am I believing that he rewards, that he is morally active on the part of those who seek him?
    Again, the truth.

If you have positively answered these questions, if you are believing what you believe, you possess a major ingredient of true success, for where faith is, there is his pleasure, and that is success.

SEVEN

Success Is Prayer

Some years ago a young man approached the foreman of a logging crew and asked for a job. "That depends," replied the foreman. "Let's see you fell this tree." The young man stepped forward and skillfully felled a great tree. Impressed, the foreman exclaimed, "Start Monday!"

Monday, Tuesday, Wednesday, Thursday rolled by, and Thursday afternoon the foreman approached the young man and said, "You can pick up your paycheck on the way out today."

Startled, he replied, "I thought you paid on Friday." "Normally we do," answered the foreman, "but we're letting you go today because you've fallen behind. Our daily felling charts show that you've dropped from first place on Monday to last on Wednesday."

"But I'm a hard worker," the young man objected. "I arrive first, leave last, and even have worked through my coffee breaks!"

The foreman, sensing the boy's integrity, thought for a minute and then asked, "Have you been sharpening your ax?"

The young man replied, *"I've been working too hard to take the time."*[1]

What an obvious mistake. How could anyone make such an unthinking error? Yet the fact is that many of

God's servants fail in their appointed tasks because they do not take time to sharpen their lives in prayer.

Indeed, when God's servants candidly talk about their spiritual lives, a majority express guilt over their prayerlessness. This means that thousands are hacking away at their ministries with increasingly dull instruments that inevitably frustrate any possible success.

We Must Pray

As God's undershepherds we must keep our lives ever sharp through prayer. John Bunyan once said: "You can do more than pray after you have prayed, but you cannot do more than pray until you have prayed."[2] Prayer is fundamental to success in the ministry.

First, we must pray because of what prayer does to us. Someone once asked George MacDonald why, if God loves us so much and knows everything we need before we ask, must we pray? MacDonald's magnificent answer remains wonderfully instructive:

> What if he knows prayer to be the thing we need first and most? What if the main object in God's idea of prayer be the supplying of our great, our endless need—the need of himself? What if the good of all our smaller and lower needs lies in this, that they help drive us to God?
>
> Communion with God is the one need of the soul beyond all other needs; prayer is the beginning of that communion.[3]

Certainly, George MacDonald is right! We have an endless need of him and prayer supplies it.

Think of it this way: our lives are like photographic plates, and prayer is like a time exposure to God. As we expose ourselves to God for a half hour, an hour, perhaps two hours a day, his image is imprinted more and more upon us. More and more we absorb the image of his char-

acter, his love, his wisdom, his way of dealing with life
and people. As servants of Christ, that is what we need
and that is what we receive from him.

Along with this, God's will is not bent to ours but ours
to his. As E. Stanley Jones says:

> Prayer is surrender—surrender to the will of God and
> cooperation with that will. If I throw out a boathook
> from the boat and catch hold of the shore and pull, do I
> pull the shore to me, or do I pull myself to the shore?
> Prayer is not pulling God to my will, but the aligning of
> my will to the will of God.[4]

Aligned with God's will, our whole person is elevated.
Thus great things become possible in our character and
actions.

Moses' experience on Mt. Sinai is the quintessential example of the benefits of such prayer. As Moses meditated
those forty days on Sinai, he was so exposed to God that
his face became radiant (Exodus 34:29-35), and his will so
bent to God's that he became the giver of the Ten Commandments. And as he went on to lead Israel, he did so in
the wisdom and way of God.

That is what we all need. It comes through spending
time with God in prayer. Are we spending enough time
for his life to be burnt into ours and our will aligned with
his? We owe it to him, to ourselves, and to the church.

*Second, we must pray because of what prayer does in the
church.* It was late in 1964 and the Communist Simba rebels had taken the town of Bunia in Zaire. They were arrest-
ing and executing any who were thought to be "enemies
of the revolution." One of their intended victims was Pastor Zebedayo Idu, who was taken from his home next to
the church. The day following his arrest was set as a great
political holiday in which speeches would be given in
front of the statue of Patrice Lumumba, the spiritual leader
of the revolution. Then large numbers of prisoners would

be executed by firing squad in front of the monument.

The next day the prisoners were herded onto a truck to be transported to their execution. But for some "mysterious reason" the engine refused to start. They were then unloaded and compelled to push-start the truck, which started only to stall again in front of the angry police commissioner's office. It was late and the furious official would have no further delay, so he lined the prisoners up and made them count off "one-two, one-two," and then ordered all the number ones to march double-time to the monument where they were killed in volleys of gunfire.

The number twos, including Pastor Zebedayo Idu, were marched back to their cell, where they listened to the firing squad and wondered why they had been spared and what the future held. Seizing the opportunity, Pastor Zebedayo shared with them the hope of eternal life. Eight prisoners trusted Christ. Hardly had the pastor finished ministering when a breathless, excited messenger came to the door with an order, "The pastor has been arrested by mistake. He is to be released at once!"

Pastor Zebedayo bade farewell to the remaining prisoners and ran to his house next to the chapel. There, gathered in the house of God, was his little congregation on their knees praying earnestly for his safety and release! Needless to say, great and long and loud was their rejoicing.[5]

How we thrill at this story of the power of prayer! And yet, it is really nothing new, for almost the exact same thing happened nearly two thousand years ago in Jerusalem when the freshly liberated Peter crashed the prayer meeting in John Mark's house, "where many people had gathered and were praying" (Acts 12:12).

Prayer brings power to the church and to ministry. It is a little-known fact that William Carey, the immensely productive "father of modern missions," had a paralyzed, bed-ridden sister who prayed for him for fifty years.

V. Raymond Edman, much-loved president of Wheaton

College, when he was a missionary in Ecuador, lay so near death that his wife actually dyed her wedding dress black for his funeral. But, thousands of miles away in Boston, Dr. Joseph Evans, unaware of Edman's plight, responded to the Spirit's direction to have his prayer group pray for Edman. They prayed desperately until Evans concluded, "Praise the Lord! The victory is won!" And, indeed, it was! For Raymond Edman recovered to go on for forty more years of remarkable service.[6]

We could go on to tell of pastors who have had "inexplicable" power in their preaching, mission outposts that have experienced unusual blessing and conversions that can be traced to the prayers of humble believers.

This is why Paul, the great apostle, pleaded: "Pray also for me, that whenever I open my mouth, words may be given me so that I will fearlessly make known the mystery of the gospel" (Ephesians 6:19). He knew that power only comes through prayer.

Third, we must pray because Jesus prayed. The Gospel of Mark tells us that as Jesus' Galilean ministry developed, he came under immense pressure from increasing multitudes. The picture he gives us is of wave upon wave of needy people coming to him—all demanding attention. So great was the press of people that Christ came into actual physical danger. Mark makes this very clear when he records that Jesus "told his disciples to have a boat ready for him, to keep the people from crowding him" (Mark 3:9). The word for "crowd" is literally the word *crush*, as the RSV translates it. It is a strange thought, but the Son of God was in danger of being crushed by the adoring crowd! So real was the danger that Jesus wisely appointed one of his disciples to wait close by in a small boat (much in the same way we would keep a car nearby with the engine running) just in case he needed to make a quick getaway. The crush of people that Jesus experienced, as Mark describes it, was comprised of those who were ill grabbing for him, the demon-possessed malevolently howling his name, and jaundiced Pharisees calculating his every move. Now that is pressure!

Jesus, though he was God, was also man and really felt the pressure. It was immense, pervasive, inescapable, and wearing, probably in ways we'll never know.

What to do? How did our Lord deal with the pressures of life and ministry? Quite simply, he did two things: first he *withdrew* to be alone, and second, he *prayed*. Of Christ's withdrawal Mark says, "He went up to the mountain." Tradition says that he ascended the Horns of Hattim, the most prominent point on the west side of the lake, and he may well have done so. But, the point is that he got away, alone, by himself. Though he was man *and* God, he still needed to be alone. Though he came to save man, he needed for a time to be away from man.

Need we say that what goes for Christ goes for us? We all need some solitude in life. Many of us never experience silence during our waking hours. We wake up to a clock radio, shave to the news, drive through noisy traffic, enter a noisy, busy office, return home listening to the rush hour reports, "relax" to the TV, and drift off to sleep as the house pulsates with the *thump, thump* of the family stereo.

We need solitude. To use the language of the mystics, we need a sanctuary, a hermitage. It's not that difficult—a church sanctuary, a parked car, the cemetery(!), a public park, a quiet living room before the family rises in the morning. Like our Master, we must regularly make the time (see Mark 1:35 and Luke 22:39). The ministry, the pressures of life, and the example of Christ demand this.

Jesus got away—that was the first step, but in doing so it always led to the greatest step. That is, he prayed. The parallel passage in Luke says, "And it was at this time that he went off to the mountains to pray, and he spent the whole night in prayer to God." There Jesus exposed his soul to the sunlight of the Father's presence. There he reaffirmed and strengthened his commitment to do the will of the Father. Such exposure, such exchange, such devotion!

The greater to the lesser logic is obvious—if Jesus had to do this while being the eternal Son, how much more do we, adopted sons and daughters, need to follow his example? Pressured servants that we are, caring people, jostled not only by the regular demands of life, but by the needy, the ill, a demonized culture, need most of all the power of prayer.

The Primacy of Prayer

Recently we stood with our sons in the armory of Cambridge University's great Fitzwilliam Museum and wondered at the ancient helmets and shields and bucklers and swords. Though these armaments were dark with the patina of centuries, we easily imagined the day when shining swords rang from their scabbards, and steel crashed against steel in awful combat. The reason for this, of course, was that every piece of armament suggested action—pounding, desperate, life-and-death action.

The same is true when we pause to reflect upon the formidable picture of the Christian warrior dressed in "the full armor of God" (Ephesians 6:12-17). Everything about it says action. He stands ready, he adjusts his war belt, repositions his helmet, gingerly tests the edge of his blade, and tensely draws his shield across his body. The enemy approaches. They stand motionless, breathing heavily. And then, the Christian soldier does the most amazing thing—he falls to his knees in deep, profound prayer! To be sure, there will be action: he will rise and his steel will flash, but all will be done in the power of prayer, for prayer is primary.

This is the precise force of the Ephesian picture, for after the Christian warrior's armament is in place, we read: "With *all* prayer and petition pray at *all* times in the Spirit, and with this in view, be on the alert with *all* perseverance and petition for *all* saints" (Ephesians 6:18, NASB, italics mine). Those who would minister for God, regardless of how well they have put on the gospel of peace, regardless of how well they wear salvation, truth, righteousness and faith, must make prayer the first thing. The Christian soldier—each person engaged in Christian ministry—fights on his knees! As Edward Payson well said:

> Prayer is the first thing, the second thing, the third thing necessary to minister. Pray, therefore, my dear brother, pray, pray, pray. [7]

The Discipline of Prayer
The call to prayer is a call to discipline. Unfortunately, many reject this idea. They argue that such thinking promotes legalism. But this simply is not so.

There is an eternity of difference between legalism and discipline. Legalism has at its core the thought of becoming better and thus gaining merit through religious exercise. Whereas discipline springs from a desire to please God. So we see that Paul, an outspoken opponent of legalism, admonishes us to discipline, as he says, ". . . discipline (literally *gymnasticize)* yourself for the purpose of godliness" (1 Timothy 4:7, NASB). God's servants must exercise themselves with an athleticlike discipline as they pursue God's purposes for their lives. There will be no prayer life without this discipline.

As we all know, it's not always easy! So the question is how do we discipline ourselves to pray? Helpfully, Dr. J. Sidlow Baxter once shared a leaf from his own pastoral diary with a group of pastors who asked just this question.

He began by telling how in 1928 he entered the ministry determined that he would be the "most Methodist-Baptist" of pastors, a real man of prayer. However, it was not long until his increasing pastoral responsibilities, administrative duties, and the subtle subterfuges of pastoral life began to crowd prayer out. He began to get used to it, making excuses for himself.

Then one morning came a crisis, as he stood over his work-strewn desk and looked at his watch. The voice of the Spirit was calling him to pray, but at the same time another velvety little voice told him to be practical and get his letters answered, that he ought to face up to the fact that he wasn't of the spiritual sort, that only a few people could be like that. That did it! "That last remark," said Baxter, "hurt like a dagger blade. I could not bear to think it was true." He was horrified by his ability to rationalize away the very ground of his ministerial vitality and power.

That morning Sidlow Baxter took a good look into his heart, and he found that there was a part of him that did not want to pray and yet a part that did. The part that didn't was his emotions, and the part that did was his intellect and will. This analysis paved the way to victory. In Dr. Baxter's own inimitable words:

As never before, my will and I stood face to face. I asked my will the straight question, "Will, are you ready for an hour of prayer?" Will answered, "Here I am, and I'm quite ready, if you are." So Will and I linked arms and turned to go for our time of prayer. At once all the emotions began pulling the other way and protesting, "We're not coming." I saw Will stagger just a bit, so I asked, "Can you stick it out, Will?" and Will replied, "Yes, if you can." So Will went, and we got down to prayer, dragging those wriggling, obstreperous emotions with us. It was a struggle all the way through. At one point, when Will and I were in the middle of an earnest intercession, I suddenly found one of those traitorous emotions had snared my imagination and had run off to the golf course; and it was all I could do to drag the wicked rascal back. A bit later I found another of the emotions had sneaked away with some off-guard thoughts and was in the pulpit, two days ahead of

schedule, preaching a sermon that I had not yet finished preparing!

At the end of that hour, if you had asked me, "Have
you had a 'good time'?" I would have had to reply, "No,
it has been a wearying wrestle with contrary emotions
and a truant imagination from beginning to end." What
is more, that battle with the emotions continued for
between two and three weeks, and if you had asked me
at the end of that period, "Have you had a 'good time'
in your daily praying?" I would have had to confess,
"No, at times it has seemed as though the heavens were
brass, and God too distant to hear, and the Lord Jesus
strangely aloof, and prayer accomplishing nothing."

Yet something *was* happening. For one thing, Will
and I really taught the emotions that we were completely independent of them. Also, one morning, about two
weeks after the contest began, just when Will and I
were going for another time of prayer, I overheard one
of the emotions whisper to the other, "Come on, you
guys, it's no use wasting any more time resisting:
they'll go just the same." That morning, for the first
time, even though the emotions were still suddenly un-
cooperative, they were at least quiescent, which allowed Will and me to get on with prayer undistractedly.

Then, another couple of weeks later, what do you
think happened? During one of our prayer times, when
Will and I were no more thinking of the emotions than
of the man in the moon, one of the most vigorous of the
emotions unexpectedly sprang up and shouted, "Halle-
lujah!" at which all the other emotions exclaimed,
"Amen!" And for the first time the whole of my being—
intellect, will, and emotions—was united in one co-
ordinated prayer-operation. All at once, God was real,
heaven was open, the Lord Jesus was luminously present, the Holy Spirit was indeed moving through my
longings, and prayer was surprisingly vital. Moreover,

in that instant there came a sudden realization that heaven had been watching and listening all the way through those days of struggle against chilling moods and mutinous emotions; also that I had been undergoing necessary tutoring by my heavenly Teacher.[8]

Fellow servants, we know that the Holy Spirit prompts us to pray, even making intercession for us, but we also know that there is our part, which is *discipline*. Surely we can do nothing in our own power; nevertheless we are called to be fellow workers with God. "Continue to work out your salvation with fear and trembling," says God's Word, "for it is God who works in you to will and to act according to his good purpose" (Philippians 2:12-13). Whatever else this requires, it requires discipline.

As we pray, we bare our souls to the light of God. He further impresses his life into ours, and our wills are drawn to his, thus sharpening the cutting edge of our lives. And this is not just prayer. It is another step on the road toward success.

As Barbara and I isolated prayer as another ingredient of true success, we were heartened. We were encouraged because we had remained committed to prayer even during our darkest times, and we were further heartened because understanding prayer from this perspective further increased our commitment to its practice.

EIGHT

Success Is Holiness

For many years he had been the honored professor of Bible at a fine Christian college. He was a vigilant guardian of biblical orthodoxy. He was an author. His encyclopedic knowledge of the Bible made him a man people looked to for wisdom. He was the confidant and advisor of college presidents, prominent pastors, and Christian executives. He was a success by everyone's estimation.

This is why we were devastated when we learned that his long association with the college had been severed because he had committed adultery. It was cause to weep—and we did.

Tragically, it was neither the first nor last occasion for tears. I have known Christian executives, celebrated speakers, and well-known pastors of churches large and small who have succumbed to sensuality.

I well remember Hudson Armerding, retired president of Wheaton College, showing me a foot-high stack of books he was reading about marriage and human relationships because he was so burdened over the failed ministries and marriages of so many of God's servants. Sensuality is a greater problem for the professional clergy than anyone actually knows. And in recent years sexual sin among Christian workers seems to have grown to epidemic proportions.

Barbara and I realized that this has telling implications

for our understanding of success in the church. The logic of Scripture is unavoidable: God calls his people to be holy (Leviticus 19:2). Holiness is foundational to true success. No one can be regarded a success who pursues a life contrary to God's will. Therefore, we came to this irony: there are untold numbers of successful pastors and Christian workers who are abysmal failures.

For those of us who would serve God, the truth is inescapable. The pursuit of holiness is essential if we are ever to know anything of real success.

Wine, Haircuts, and Dead Men

The Old Testament is filled with extraordinarily graphic accounts of failed lives, perhaps none more tragic than the story of Samson.

The background for Samson's story is summarized in this final refrain from the Book of Judges, "Everyone did what was right in his own eyes." It was one of the darkest times in Israel's history, a time of gross idolatry and brutal oppression by alien powers. This great darkness was the reason for God's call to Samson, for it was God's intention to use this remarkably gifted young man to deliver Israel from the heel of the Philistines.

God's call came before the birth of Samson. And of his life it can be truly said that there have been few born with greater expectations. The announcement of his birth came through multiple angelic annunciations (Judges 13). Quite naturally, when word of the angel of the Lord's appearance to Samson's barren parents spread through the tribe of Dan, expectations soared. These expectations were enhanced when, in obedience to the angel's instructions, Samson's mother-to-be became a Nazarite, and then also Samson at birth. The significance of their Nazarite status was understood by all to mean that they were set apart as "holy to the Lord." Their commitment was symbolized by the commitment to abstain from alcohol, cutting the hair, and touching a dead body (Numbers 6:1-8).[1]

Thus, from birth, all eyes were upon the Nazarite boy, and as he grew to manhood, none could mistake his calling as his unshorn hair draped ever longer across his broad shoulders. Moreover, when Samson's athletic frame passed by, a thrill of expectation coursed through the people. *What is God going to do,* they wondered, *with this young man who has been set apart as holy from the womb?* Though it must not be overdrawn, there is an instructive parallel here for all those who have received a call to ministry, as it is primarily a call to *holiness,* and a call which brings with it *high spiritual expectations.* This is why what happens to Samson is so relevant to those who would succeed in serving God.

Wine, Women, and Song
The Bible makes it clear that by early manhood Samson was failing in his holy commitment. The young man became consumed by sensuality. The very first description of him is that he burned with erotic passion. Samson *sees* one of the Philistine women and immediately returns to his parents, demanding over their objections that they arrange a wedding. There is no record that he had even spoken with the woman. But he prevailed, and as the Scripture says, "He went down and talked to the woman, and she looked good to Samson" (Judges 14:7, NASB). Thus began the first of a number of affairs.

If Samson was in the grip of sensuality, sensuality was equally held in his hot grasp. Samson wouldn't let go. He never got beyond his libidinal adolescence, and because of this he successively broke his Nazarite vows, completely undoing his commitment to holiness and his call—and assuring his downfall.

First, in pursuing his romance with the Philistine woman, Samson returned to the dried carcass of a lion and scooped out wild honey from its cavity. This was a blatant transgression of his commitment not to go near a dead body.

Next Samson transgressed his vow regarding strong drink when he prepared a "feast" for a stag party celebrating his upcoming wedding to the girl (Judges 14:10). The Hebrew word for "feast" lays stress on the fact that there was plenty to drink, and of course, the implication is that Samson drank his fair share.[2]

Moral Valium
As we all know, the ultimate desecration of Samson's holy vows came from the cutting of his hair. What is remarkable here is Samson's amazing *desensitization* to his spiritual state and the danger he was in. Evidently the previous experience of God's power in his life had given him a childish sense of invincibility. This can be the only explanation for the repeated frivolous exchanges with his mistress Delilah, who was clearly trying to kill him! This is the only explanation for his final stupidity in revealing to her the secret of his strength. And this is the explanation that the Bible gives after the fatal shearing: "Then she called, 'Samson, the Philistines are upon you!' He awoke from his sleep and thought, 'I'll go out as before and shake myself free.' But he did not know that the Lord had left him" (Judges 16:20). What a terrible, terrible pronouncement! And it is even more terrible today because it is being repeated in the lives of thousands of God's servants. For many it is a ministerial epitaph: "But he did not know that the Lord had departed from him."

Today's Samsons
Samson's failure is relevant, for as we have seen, many of God's servants who once responded to the call of God and committed themselves to a holy life and went forth with great expectations have fallen to sensuality. Right now, some who have been instruments of great power are still continuing in active ministry, though knee-deep in sensuality. Some have become so morally desensitized that they do not know that the Lord has departed from them. They

are, by God's own definition, successful failures.

The failure of Samson is a warning to God's present-day servants who live in a culture that oozes sex from all its pores. Samson's failure poses for us some tough questions:

1. Are we being desensitized by the present evil world? Do things that once shocked us now pass by with little notice? Have our own sexual ethics slackened?

2. Where do our minds wander when we have no duties to perform?

3. What are we reading? Are there books or magazines or files in our libraries that we want no one else to see?

4. What are we renting at the local video stores? How many hours do we spend watching TV? How many adulteries did we watch last week? How many murders? How many did we watch with our children?

5. How many chapters of the Bible did we read last week?

I have asked these hard questions because there is a cloud of sensuality that oppresses everyone. And what makes it even worse is the amazing human capacity for self-delusion. The human personality has an innate capacity to rationalize and compartmentalize its morality. I have known Christ-professing, Bible-carrying men and women in Christian ministry who were adulterous, even incestuous, and saw no contradiction in their lives. I have known Christian workers who have led a secret pornographic existence: fundamentalists at church and X-rated cable voyeurs at home. Even more tragic, their delusion is so deep that they admit no inconsistency in their behavior. How Samson-like!

But God's word stands: all is failure apart from holiness. This is what Samson's failure teaches us. It is also the message of David's failure, as we now shall see.

The Rise and Fall of Camelot

King David was not an obvious candidate for failure. He had united all of Israel and was at the zenith of his personal power. It was Camelot, the real Camelot! But he did fall. And his fall (next to that of Adam and Eve) was the greatest in history because he fell from such dizzying heights.

David's success, however, should not be interpreted to mean that his reign was without its problems. There were definite flaws in his conduct that left him open to disaster.

Second Samuel 5, which records David's assumption of power in Jerusalem, mentions almost as an aside that "After he left Hebron, David took more concubines and wives in Jerusalem" (2 Samuel 5:13). We must note, and note it well, that *David's taking of wives was sin*. Deuteronomy 17, which sets down the standards for the Hebrew kings, commands that they refrain from three things: (1) acquiring many horses, (2) taking many wives, and (3) accumulating much silver and gold. David did fine on one and three, but he completely failed on number two when he collected a considerable harem.

Here we must observe that a progressive *desensitization* to sin and consequent descent from holiness was already taking place in David's life. David's collection of wives, though it was "legal" and not considered adultery in the culture of the day, was sin, nevertheless. And like Samson, David's sensual indulgence desensitized him to God's holy call on his life as well as to the dangers and consequences of falling. In short, David's embrace of sensuality desensitized him to God's call and made him easy prey for the fatal sin of his life.

David's Look of Lust

It had been a warm day, and evening was falling. So the king strode out on his rooftop garden for some cool evening air and a look at his city at dusk. As he gazed, his eye caught the form of an unusually beautiful woman—bathing without embarrassment. As to how beautiful she was, the Hebrew is explicit: the woman was "beautiful of appearance, very" (2 Samuel 11:2). She was young, in the flower of life. And the evening shadows made her even more enticing.

The king looked. And he continued to look. After the first glance, David should have turned the other way and retired to his chamber. But he did not, and his *look* became a *stare* and then a *leer*.

Lay this maxim to heart: *When lust takes control, God is quite unreal to us.* What a world of wisdom there is in this! When we are in the grip of lust, the reality of God fades. The longer King David gazed, the less real God became. Not only was his awareness of God diminished, but in the growing darkness he lost awareness of who David was— his holy call, his frailty, and the sure consequences of sin.

That is what lust does. It has done it millions of times. Lust makes God disappear, at least in the lust-glazed eyes of those involved. Here, fellow servants, we must once again ask some questions: Is God fading from view? Were you once walking close with him, but now, because of creeping sensuality, he seems but a distant phantom? If so, you must take decisive steps to guard your heart. You must terminate the intake of lustful words and images— whether they be gotten from reading, or the media, or an acquaintance. If you do not, God will fade and you will fall.

David's Rationalization

When King David's intent became apparent to his servants, one tried to dissuade him, saying, "Isn't this Bathsheba, the daughter of Eliam, the wife of Uriah the Hittite?" But David would not be rebuffed.

Certainly some massive rationalizing took place in David's mind, just as J. Allan Petersen has suggested in *The Myth of the Greener Grass:*

Uriah is a great soldier but he's probably not much of a husband or a lover—years older than she is—and he'll be away for a long time. This girl needs a little comfort in her loneliness. This is one way I can help her. No one will get hurt. I don't mean anything wrong by it. This is not lust—I've known that many times. This is love. This is not the same as finding a prostitute on the street. God knows that. And to the servant, "Bring her to me."[3]

The mind controlled by lust has, it seems, an infinite capacity for rationalization:

- "This marriage was never God's will in the first place."
- "God's will is for me to be happy; certainly he would not deny me anything which is essential to my happiness."
- "How can something which has brought so much good be wrong?"
- "The bottom line is love—and I'm acting on the basis of the highest law."
- "Christians and their judgmental attitudes make me sick. You're judging me. You're a greater sinner than I am!"

Such are rationalizations of those who once served God with all their hearts, who are still, perhaps, successful failures.

David's Adultery and Its Consequences

David, the great heart, the greatest among men, fell. And great was his fall. David was unaware that he had stepped off the precipice and unaware of his plunge. But the reality would soon arrive. The bottom was coming up fast.

If David could have seen the consequences of transgressing God's holiness, he would never have taken the fatal step.

We are all familiar with David's despicable behavior in arranging Uriah's murder to cover his sin. Suffice it to say that at this time Uriah was a better man drunk than David was sober! (2 Samuel 11:13). A year later David would repent under the withering accusation of the prophet Nathan. But the damage was already done. The miserable consequences could not be undone.

As has been often pointed out:

■ It was the breaking of the *tenth* commandment, coveting his neighbor's wife, that led David to commit adultery, thus breaking the *seventh* commandment.

■ Then, in order to steal his neighbor's wife (thereby breaking the *eighth* commandment), he committed murder and broke the *sixth* commandment.

■ He broke the *ninth* commandment by bearing false witness against his brother.

■ This all brought dishonor to his parents and thus broke the *fifth* commandment.

In this way he broke all the commandments that relate to loving one's neighbor as oneself. And in all of this he dishonored God as well. *There is no such thing as a simple sin!*[4] Oh, if only all God's servants could see this and believe it!

From here on David's reign went downhill, despite his laudable repentance. Here are the terrible facts. His baby died. Then his beautiful daughter, Tamar, was raped by her half-brother Amnon. In turn, Amnon was murdered by Tamar's full-brother Absalom. Absalom so came to hate his father David for his moral turpitude that he led a rebellion under the tutelage of Bathsheba's resentful grandfather, Ahithophel.

David's reign lost the smile of God. His throne never regained its former stability.

David's fall stands as a mournful warning to all those who would follow God. There is no success without holiness.

Understand, servants of God, that some of life's choices, especially those that have to do with sensuality, have irreversible consequences. You may be making that choice now. For your sake and for God's sake, do not take the fatal step. Repent!

Samson's Epitaph

The logic of Scripture cannot be circumvented: God's will for his people is to be holy, thus no one can be regarded a success who lives contrary to his will. Holiness is fundamental to true success. Holiness must be our preoccupation, our earnest pursuit.

Admittedly, there is more to holiness than sexual purity, but in today's libidinous culture sexual sin has been one of the main avenues of transgression, as is attested by the litany of disasters among God's servants. That is why we emphasize its danger so.

Brothers and sisters, we must not allow our increasingly pornographic culture to draw us away from our call to holiness. We must not allow sensuality to drug us so that, like Samson, we do not know that the Lord has departed from us. What a terrible, terrible epitaph! Lust makes God fade from our view, and along with that goes a concern for his holiness. Our sensual minds then form incredible rationalizations, and we lose all sense of who we are and the inevitable consequences. We become failures, for we become like immoral Esau whose sensual fixation drove him to sell his magnificent calling for a simple meal. The Christian ministry is littered with Esaus.

Barbara and I learned that if we were to be accorded success in the ministry, we had to pursue lives of holiness. This meant that we had to follow the example of Job, who said, "I made a covenant with my eyes not to look lustfully at a girl" (Job 31:1). By God's power we must covenant not to view anything that would pull us down from holiness to sensuality, whether in printed material, in the media, or in life.

I made this covenant as a teenager. And I can say it is one of the most healthy, sanctifying, holy promises I have ever made.

During our difficult time in learning about success, Barbara and I were encouraged as we came to see that holiness is foundational to true success. We were also heartened. Although holiness is not easy, the fact that God demands it means that he helps those who seek it.

NINE

Success Is Attitude

When the following letter came to the Hughes household, it brought a sigh of relief and repeated chuckles. It was a form letter response to a note of encouragement I had written some months before to a friend who had suffered a heart attack.

Dear Kent, et al.,
Following my recent heart attack, the doctors informed me that there was one chance in ten that within six months I would have a second attack which would be fatal and one chance in five that I would have another nonfatal attack. With the realization that these were lousy odds, I decided to wait the six months to answer all the cards and messages I had received from so many concerned friends and acquaintances. I figured if things went well statistically I might never have to answer, or could answer once for two "hits."

Well, the six months are up. The odds are now getting better and better that I'll die of something else so I'm forced to respond. My excuses for being inconsiderate are all used up.

Thank you for your concern.
Thank you for your message.
Thank you for your caring.
Thank you for your love.

Each message received was one more good reason to fight. Without them the struggle would have been almost unbearable.

I've lost 35 pounds. I'm jogging five miles a day in under 60 minutes (and hating every minute of it). I can have anything I want to eat as long as I don't put salt on it and don't swallow it. No meat, no dairy products, no nothin' but vegetables, fruits, grains, and a restricted amount of nuts. (As you know, no matter how you cook them, vegetables are really inedible.)

May I suggest: Don't get old . . . you'll live to regret it.

My love,
John

What an upbeat, encouraging letter! John's resurgent wit and humor told us that he was feeling better. But even more, it revealed a healthy attitude. And that was most heartening because there is a sense in which *attitude is everything*. Our physicians tell us this is so when they remind us that a high percentage of illnesses are produced by unhealthy mind-sets and attitudes.

The influence of positive mental attitude is not limited to medicine. Today "attitude" is virtually a sports cliché. Attitude, we are told, separates the greats from the also–rans. Similarly, educators, marriage counselors, corporate managers, military brass—all assert the importance of attitude.

In Christian ministry it is no exaggeration to say (with some common-sense qualifications, of course) that attitude is everything. There are two attitudes that particularly characterize ministerial failures: negativism and jealousy.

For Barbara and myself, an honest look at our attitudes was indispensable in determining whether our lives were moving toward success or failure. Here are some of the things we learned.

A Positive or Negative Attitude?

Prison for the Apostle Paul should have been an exquisitely frustrating experience. He was a "type A" personality if there ever was one—and his goal was nothing less than the evangelization of the entire Gentile world! He was the missionary general of the early church. He had led the way in evangelizing Turkey; he was the first missionary to Greece; he had battled the Judaizers in Jerusalem and across Asia and won!

Paul labored night and day for the church. He was eminently brave as, for example, when he reentered Lystra after being stoned by its inhabitants (Acts 14:6-8). And he had such compassion for his own people that he honestly could cry, "I could wish myself cut off that they might be saved!" What a supercharged heart! But this heart was locked up in Rome, in the "slammer," under house arrest.

And on top of all this, he was suffering opposition from those who claimed the name of Christ. Of them he says, "It is true that some preach Christ out of envy and rivalry . . . not sincerely, supposing that they can stir up trouble for me while I am in chains" (Philippians 1:15-17). With Paul out of the way, immature, selfish, would-be church leaders were doing everything they could to increase their personal prominence by preaching the gospel. Paul had become victim of what would be called the *odium theologicum*, the hatred of theologians, the malice of those within the church who jealously covet another's influence and power.

Humanly speaking, things could not have been much more difficult. And this is to say nothing about his thorn in the flesh (2 Corinthians 12:7-8). How natural it would have been for Paul to cry, "What's going on, God? I've given my life to you, and I've paid the price willingly. But now, just when I'm needed most, here I am in this hole. My best years are wasting, Lord! I can't stand it!" But not

Paul. Listen to his personal assessment of the situation: "But what does it matter? The important thing is that in every way, whether from false motives or true, Christ is preached. And because of this I rejoice" (Philippians 1:18).

Paul displays a remarkably positive attitude in the midst of his impossible situation. Moreover, he indicates that this is a matter of his own choice: "In this I rejoice, yes, and I *will* rejoice." Paul chose to have a positive attitude during his imprisonment, a fact that the joyous tone of his Philippian letter attests from beginning to end. Attitude makes all the difference in the world.

My wife's dear friend, Cloe Ann Voll, had had a terrible year. A lump in her breast was found to be malignant and her breast was removed. Then began the unpleasant process of chemotherapy. She felt extremely ill and cruelly maimed. Each day she faced the reality of yet another indignity—more and more of her hair was falling out, and she was growing bald.

My wife, of course, had made several trips from our home in Chicago to the Voll's in Minneapolis, but we all desperately wanted to get together. So we planned a rendezvous at a friend's vacation home halfway between us near Madison. I will never forget the night we arrived. The Volls arrived first. Bob had proceeded to fix dinner for us all, and as we stepped from our car a welcome aroma invited us to the door. There we were greeted by a smiling, buoyant, *bald* Cloe Ann. Having tired of her wig, she had discarded it and taped a great pink bow in its place! Never, to Barbara and me, had she been more lovely. We'll never forget that night with all its laughter, joy, and tears.

The secret ingredient, of course, was Cloe Ann's attitude. She didn't spend the evening recounting what she didn't have. She didn't dwell on what she had lost. She concentrated on what she had!

That's how it was with Paul. To be sure, he was in jail, sure others were preaching out of spite and selfish ambition, sure he was confined and uncomfortable, sure he had lost his health; but he had Christ who loved him, he had salvation, and he had a great future—for his citizenship was in heaven. Paul knew that God could deliver him any time in any way, if he wished to do so. Paul knew that God's sovereign plan would be worked out in his life and that of the church regardless of what man might do—and he was confident in the future.

Next to our free salvation in Christ, our attitude is the most important thing we possess. Attitude is more important than circumstances, the past, money, successes, failures, our gifts, other's opinions, even the "facts."

We all have a choice every day regarding the attitude with which we will embrace the day. It is up to us to make a positive volitional choice. A positive attitude, like Paul's in prison, is a solid step toward success.

> *Two men looked through the bars.*
> *One saw the mud, the other, the stars.*[1]

What do you see?

Jealous Detractors, Loving Encouragers

The Book of Numbers tells us that when Joshua was serving as assistant to Moses, he received disconcerting news. Some elders named Eldad and Medad were prophesying (preaching) in the camp of Israel! To Joshua this was an affront to Moses' spiritual leadership, for Moses was Israel's prophet *par excellence.* Alarmed, and jealous for Moses, Joshua immediately went to him, blurting, "Moses, my lord, stop them!" fully expecting Moses to take action. But to Joshua's great surprise, Moses replied, "Are you jealous for my sake? I wish that all the Lord's people were prophets and that the Lord would put his Spirit on them!" (Numbers 11:28-29).

It was a watershed experience for Joshua. Had he not been checked here, his "selfless jealousy" for Moses' honor could have eventually made him a narrow, petty man, unfit for ministry. As it turned out, the lesson was well-learned; Joshua never again displayed such smallness, and he became a man who lived only for God's glory.

For those in God's service, Joshua's error spotlights one of the most deadly traps of all: *ministerial jealousy*. It is a sin that has ensnared the most accomplished Christian men and women.

An ancient story from the fourth century tells of inexperienced demons finding great difficulty in tempting a godly hermit. They lured him with every manner of temptation, but he could not be enticed. Frustrated, the imps returned to Satan and recited their plight. He responded that they had been far *too hard* on the monk. "Send him a message," he said, "that his brother has just been made bishop of Antioch. Bring him *good* news." Mystified by the devil's advice, the demons nevertheless returned and dutifully reported the wonderful news to the hermit. And, in that very instant, he fell—into deep, wicked jealousy.

How true this is to human experience! As St. John of the Cross put it: "As far as envy is concerned, many experience displeasure when they see others in possession of spiritual goods. They feel sensibly hurt because others surpass them on this road, and they resent it when others are praised."[2]

As we have noted in Paul's life, this was something of what motivated the sinful competition of his colleagues while he languished in prison. It also spurred John the Baptist's disciples to warn John of Jesus' rising star and the danger of eclipse as they told him "everyone is going to him" (John 3:26). The same pernicious cloud blankets much of the ministry today. John Claypool said in his 1979 Yale Lecture on Preaching that even while in seminary he experienced jealous jockeying for position, and that his experience in the parish ministry had not been much different. He writes:

I can still recall going to state and national conventions in our denomination and coming home feeling drained and unclean, because most of the conversation in the hotel rooms and the halls was characterized either by envy of those who were doing well or scarcely concealed delight for those who were doing poorly. For did that not mean that someone was about to fall, and thus create an opening higher up the ladder?[3]

The problem is immense, and the immensity demands honesty. Frankly, how do we *feel* when a colleague has gone to a prestigious church? Or written a fine book? Or been asked to preach at the annual convention? Or been praised by someone from whom we have desired praise? Or perhaps even more revealing, how do we feel when we hear of a colleague's weakness, or misfortune, or humbling?

Pygmy hearts undermine personal success, do they not?

Besides this, jealous, envious hearts are unhappy, for there is a miserable pathology to jealousy. The Bible unforgettably commemorates this in the case of the prodigal's older brother. His jealous heart makes it impossible for him to share in his family's joy. In fact, he misses the party of his life! (Luke 14:25-30). Then, unable to share in the things that please his father, he suffers further estrangement. His brother becomes to him "this son of yours" (Luke 15:30). He is out of sync not only with his brother but his father. He is miserable. A heart subject to such pathology can never be successful, regardless of its outward performance.

How much better to be a loving encourager rather than a jealous detractor! How much better to be like Moses—"I wish that all the Lord's people were prophets and that the Lord would put his Spirit on them!" (Numbers 11:29). How much better to be like Jonathan who "made a covenant with David because he loved him as himself" and committed his life to making David king (1 Samuel 18:1-4)! How very much better to be like John the Baptist who responded to his disciples' warning of Jesus' ascendance over him saying, "A man can receive only what is given him from heaven. . . . He must become greater; I must become less" (John 3:27-30). *There* is a successful man! At least Jesus thought so, for he said, "I tell you the truth: Among those born of women there has not risen anyone greater than John the Baptist" (Matt. 11:11).

Is such a life possible today? Of course! Just as it was for Charles Simeon, the great preacher of Kings' College and Holy Trinity Church, Cambridge. Hugh Evan Hopkins, his biographer, tells that:

> When in 1808 Simeon's health broke down and he had to spend some eight months recuperating on the Isle of Wight, it fell to Thomason to step into the gap and preach as many as five times on a Sunday in Trinity Church and Stapleford. He surprised himself and everyone else by developing a preaching ability almost equal to his vicar's, at which Simeon, totally free from any suggestion of professional jealousy, greatly rejoiced. He quoted the Scripture, "He must increase; but I must decrease," and told a friend, "Now I see why I have been laid aside. I bless God for it."[4]

Such a life, such success, is available to the honest person who will ask God for it, because such is God's will for each of his servants.

"If one part is honored, every part rejoices with it" (1 Corinthians 12:26). When another has success, we have success!

An encouraging attitude is success in itself.

Savoring the Sweetness of Life
The concerned son of a prominent pastor sat in my study and spoke candidly, "My father is retired now, but he's

just as resentful and unhappy as he has always been." Surprised at this grim epitaph, I gently probed for the reason. The young man went on to describe how his well-thought-of, "workaholic" father always felt he was just a step from failure and humiliation. Expecting the worst (which, incidentally, never came), he literally married himself to the church, all the while disliking the people he served, and envious of his colleagues who had it "better" than he.

What a contrast with the pastor I met in a remote little western town. His church met in rented facilities and his car had seen better days, as had his trailer-house home. But as we walked down Main Street, stepping around the tumbleweeds, he remarked, "I can't believe how good God is to me. I have a wonderful wife, a church to serve, and sunshine 365 days a year!" And then he spent the day helping me set up a weeklong outreach.

Those who have negative attitudes in the ministry never truly know success, regardless of their accomplishments. Their negativism sours the proper sweetness of their desserts. Nothing tastes right. They are unable to enjoy the pleasant things that come their way, for they always manage to dwell on what might have been and fear the worst in what is to come. Such attitudes naturally lead to jealousy, which envies the good fortunes of others, or finds satisfaction in their misfortunes. This miserable pattern further excludes one from the experience of success.

Those caught in this vicious negative critical syndrome please neither God nor themselves.

On the other hand, those with a Pauline attitude are always seeing the stars, even through the bars. They are hopeful regarding the future, and very often they are the ones God uses to forward his plan.

These servants are naturally the encouragers of God's people. They are like Moses and Jonathan and Charles Simeon and Alexander Whyte, of whom it was said, "All of his geese became swans"—for such was the elevating effect of his friendship to his fellow pastors.

Through the example of Paul and others, Barbara and I became aware of how important a role our mind-set played in our ministry. We had learned that a *positive* attitude and an *encouraging* attitude are foundational to a truly successful life. Now we strive to put this discovery into practice.

TEN

Sweet Success!

Kent and I enjoyed arriving early for Sunday evening service at the community center where we held our worship services. Our boys liked it because they could use the playground equipment in the adjacent park; the girls liked it because they could help Mom and Dad "check things out" and greet those dependables who came early to help. Kent and I felt especially good because we had been thinking through this matter of success, and our burden had noticeably lightened.

Soon the hall was in good order, the boys were corralled on one side of me and the girls sat on the other side. Kent had taken his chair up front. There was only one problem. Hardly anyone was there; perhaps ten, at the most.

Kent, of course, ignored the empty seats and after the opening greeting and prayer began a lively, though embarrassingly weak, time of singing. There simply were not enough good voices to fill the hall. A few latecomers straggled in, which helped considerably to bolster the singing. The special music was excellent, and this was followed by a moving testimony by one of the men. But when Kent got up to preach, there were only twenty-five in attendance, half of whom were children, four of whom were our own! Hardly a banner night!

In the past, we would have been discouraged by this. Kent, particularly, would have become depressed and self-doubting. But not on this night. As Kent stood in the pulpit to preach his message, he looked over at me and a silent communication passed between us. And I prayed what I sensed was on Kent's heart: *Thank you, God, for these twenty-five dear people. What a privilege it is to serve them here!*

That evening, I saw a new man in Kent. I sensed that he somehow had been freed. Indeed, he had been. The pressures of the success syndrome had been lifted from him, and it seemed he had eased back into the freedom we all have in Christ.

We had discovered that the miserable yoke of worldly success is so crushing because it is a burden that God's servants were never meant to bear.

Success in a Small Church

So this is our testimony: *we found success in a small church that was not growing. We found success in the midst of what the world would call failure.*

Nothing had changed in our situation. The circumstances that had so paralyzed us those weeks before had not changed. If anything, they had intensified. But we had changed.

In our study of the Scriptures, Kent and I had learned that we are not called to success, as the world fancies it, but to *faithfulness.* We realized that the results are for God and eternity to reveal. This basic understanding made possible the succeeding discoveries about God's view of success, which we have shared with you.

We're not suggesting that on that day we had perfectly analyzed success and put it all together. But we had simply come to see the basic plan for biblical success. To the best of our ability we were striving:

1. To be faithful (obedient to God's Word and hardworking)
2. To serve God and others
3. To love God
4. To believe he *is* (to believe what we believe)

5. To pray
6. To pursue holiness
7. To develop a positive attitude

This was our liberation and, may we humbly say, our success.

That night when we repacked our "church" into the storage trailer, lugging microphones, hymnals, playpens, and rockers from the community center, we were filled with joy. And when we were home, and the children were tucked in, Kent and I sat together in our kitchen with our coffee cups in our hands and talked and talked far into the night.

What a change from that other dark night! It was one of the great times of our lives.

The Lesson Wears Well

It has been years now since that crucial night, but what we experienced has been an anchor to our ministry.

Later when we moved to College Church in Wheaton and it began to grow, we were excited to be a part of the growth, but actually it meant less to us than some would expect. In our hearts we knew, and we continue to know, that we may never be more successful than we were that Sunday night in our struggling church with twenty-five people.

We have come to understand that, as we minister, God our Father sees us and our success in ways we cannot readily see ourselves.

An experience from our time as parents of young children helped us see something of this. The school was presenting its annual Christmas program. Two of our children had parts in their class plays. Holly, our eighth-grader, had the lead of Della in O'Henry's *The Gift of the Magi*, and our fourth-grader, Kent, had four lines as a Wise Man in the Christmas pageant.

Holly's play came first, and she was terrific! She had her lines down cold and she articulated them perfectly, projecting them so that the whole auditorium could hear. And she *was* dramatic—moving about the stage as a perfect nineteenth-century heroine, at times her hands extended imploringly, then her wrist to her head in a dither. She stole the show. And when it was over, we proudly joined the chorus of applause.

Later came Kent's play. He had been working on his four lines since Thanksgiving and had found it difficult to remember them. Not only that, but he was terrified of the stage. Still, we shall never forget the moment he stood in his shepherd's costume with his black tennies showing beneath the hem of his white robe, his eyes saucerwide with stage fright, and his hands repeatedly flexing at his sides. We held our breath as we heard him say,

> *Strange feelings come upon me*
> *Though I know not why.*
> *The night is still around me,*
> *The stars shine in the sky.*

There was no way we could applaud. It was the middle of the play. But our hearts applauded and applauded. How pleased we were—with both of our children!

And so we came to better understand that God is not so interested in our being the star of the show as much as he is that we do our best with the part he has given us. In terms of ministry, it's not whether we minister to twenty-five or twenty-five hundred that determines success. Rather, it is what we are doing with the role he has given us.

The marvelous truth is that whether famous or nameless, prominent or unknown, great or small, God's principles for success remain the same, and success is *equally* available to all. God has not placed success out of reach. He does not dangle it, tantalizing but impossible, before us. Success is possible for everyone. Anyone can be a success in God's eyes.

The Questions of Success

We recommend that if at all possible you retire to a place alone to consider the following questions.[1] We suggest you prayerfully set yourself before God and answer them as if they were audibly coming from his lips, realizing that he knows all things.

1. Are you proving faithful in the exercise of your ministry? Specifically, are you *obedient* to God's Word? Or is there, perhaps, some area, in personal or public ministry, in which you are knowingly disobedient? (This is a telling question because you cannot be a faithful servant and a disobedient servant at the same time.) Also, since there can be no such thing as a faithful but lazy servant, are you truly hardworking?

2. Are you living your life as a servant, or have you drifted from servanthood into self-service? The question is fundamental to success, for this will move you from success to failure.

3. The great question for all who want to please God is, Do we love him? After his resurrection, Jesus unforgettably dramatized this question by asking Peter three times, "Do you love me?" Thus, from the lips of Jesus we learn that nothing is of greater importance! There can be no success without loving God.

4. Do we believe that God's Son is the *Creator* of everything in the universe, *Sustainer* of every atom, the *Goal* of all creation, and the *Lover* of our souls who died for us? And more, do we believe that as *Rewarder* he will equitably reward us? We *say* we believe it. But do we really believe it with all our hearts? *Do we believe what we believe?* If so, we have the smile of God, and that is true success.

5. Are we people of prayer? Do we regularly take significant portions of time for an exposure to God, to bare our needs and the needs of our people to God? Is your prayer life moving toward success or failure?

6. Is your life growing in holiness? Or are you becoming captive to the culture? In respect to holiness, would God classify your life as a success or a failure? There is much to consider here. But this question is so important to the Christian life and ministry; it must be answered.

7. What is your basic attitude toward your ministry—positive or negative? Some attitudes exclude success, namely negativism and jealousy. Negative people never fully experience success, regardless of their accomplishment. Their negativism taints their work for God and the experience of satisfaction they might have enjoyed. Jealous people envy the good fortune of others and gloat over others' misfortunes. They find it difficult to rejoice with those who rejoice. Such people please neither God nor themselves. But those with positive, encouraging attitudes are a success in themselves for they serve God with a heart that pleases him—and that is success.

Now that you have meditated on the questions of success, we hope that you are encouraged. For again, whether you sense that you are on the upside or downside of the questions, one thing ought to be even more clear by your having considered them: *Success is within your reach.* It makes no difference whether your ministry is sailing or struggling, whether it is large or small, prominent or obscure; you can be a success and know it!

Our prayer is that in seeing where success lies, and knowing where you stand, you will be liberated to pursue your part in God's work with joyful release.

Blessed Mediocrity

We are aware that it is possible to suppose that by refusing to quantify success (as for example, by size of congregation and staff, or numbers of souls won, or books in print, or degrees, or breadth of influence and prestige) we are encouraging mediocrity.

Far from it! Instead, think of what it would mean if we were *faithful*, living in profound obedience to God's Word and working long and hard at our tasks; *serving* with a foot-washing heart; *loving* God with all our heart, soul, and might; *believing* what we believe; *praying* with the dependence and passion of Christ; living pure *holy* lives in this sensual world; manifesting a positive, supportive *attitude* in the midst of difficulties! If that is mediocrity, then give us more of this blessed mediocrity—for it is success!

PART THREE

ENCOURAGEMENTS

ELEVEN

Encouragement from God

As long as I live I shall never forget the night I candidated at College Church in Wheaton. It was August 5, 1979, and it was a typically hot, muggy midwestern day in the nineties. I had preached the morning services and they were wonderfully uneventful. Everything had gone well.

But the evening service was a far different story. It was much hotter than the morning and even more humid because a thunderstorm was brewing. I was heavily perspiring as I sat on the platform in the old Georgian-style sanctuary, though I had not spoken a word.

I was having second thoughts about the passage I had chosen to speak on. It was Luke 8, which tells the story of Jesus healing the woman who had the issue of blood. I had selected it because the previous week I had casually asked my children what I should preach on—and that was their suggestion. They liked the sermon because it included a story about one of their friends. Hardly a reason to choose a text for a candidating sermon!

As I looked down I saw three couples whom I had heard and read about for years. Their leadership in various Christian organizations was well known. They sat side by side on the front right row—Ken and Margaret Taylor, Dave and Phyllis Howard, and Joe and Mary Lou Bayly. They were close enough to see me perspire. I remember saying under my breath, "What in the world am I doing here? And why did I choose this text?" But I hid everything (I think!) behind a benign, ecclesiastical smile.

That was just the beginning of a long night! As I announced my text and began to preach, I could see through the open windows the skies turn a telltale cyclone green, and it began to pour. It rained so hard I had to raise my voice and stay close to the mike to be adequately heard. Then it began to thunder, and lightning started to flash brightly outside. Sweating even more, I calmly continued my candidating sermon, all the while saying to myself, "I can't believe this . . . Lord help me!"

Then—a simultaneous flash and boom, and the College Church fire alarm sounded! Now, I must tell you that the College Church fire alarm is not a dainty bell, nor is it even an obtrusive buzzer. It is a deafening horn which sounds very much like it belongs to a diesel truck. People gasped. My oldest daughter, Holly, jumped to her feet, sure a tornado was on its way. The presiding pastor took the microphone, assuring the congregation that there was nothing to worry about—that the sensitive ionization alarm was set to sound if there was a lightning strike nearby—and then he turned the pulpit back to me.

I told the people that if I ever wrote a book this story would be in it, and I continued to sweat and preach a sermon punctuated *twenty-two* more times by the horn, as the alarm kept shorting out! All this not to mention the arrival of fire trucks with their sirens howling and lights blinking!

When I closed in prayer and descended the platform, I was exhausted! I had perspired so much even the shoulders of my suit coat were wet. If that were not enough, I greeted people at the reception in the church basement with wet feet—the basement had suffered a minor flood during the deluge. I sincerely thought that this was "it" for me and College Church. As I greeted the congregation one by one, I kept thinking, *Nice to meet you. Too bad I won't be seeing you again.*

But, as is often the case, I was wrong. The people thought that if I could survive that, I could handle anything. "Besides," they said, "we want a man who can call down fire from heaven!"

Two weeks later they voted to call me as their pastor.

The Trauma of New Beginnings

New beginnings in the pastorate are traumatic for any pastor and family. Suddenly he has a whole new sea of faces and names to learn—and to love. He wonders if his children are going to be accepted by those in the youth group. If not, there is nowhere else for them to go. He does not know whether the people will like his preaching, or how his leadership style will be accepted. Quite simply, he wonders if he and the congregation will "click."

I felt all these pressures and concerns in the beginning, and only my wife knew what I was dealing with. At least I thought she was the only one. There was someone else, however—Bob Noles, the West Coast Representative for Wheaton College—who had recommended me for the job, a man with pastoral experience himself.

Bob invited me to lunch at a local restaurant, and there, after some gentle probing, he said in his warm pastoral way, "Kent, I want to share a verse with you that has meant so much to Renee and me," and he opened his Bible to Jeremiah 29:11 and read these words: "'For I know the plans I have for you,' declares the Lord, 'plans for welfare and not for calamity, to give you a future and a hope'" (NASB).

From these words, Bob Noles assured me that whatever came, whether severity or goodness, God had plans for my welfare. I took this verse to my heart in those early months. It has become dear to all my thinking and my outlook on life.

The promise was first given to the Jews at the beginning of their seventy years of Babylonian captivity as an encouragement to remain faithful. But it applies in principle to us because, as people of faith who desire to please God, we share in a blessed continuity of faith and application. So I share it with you, my comrades in ministry, because life in Christian service is a series of new beginnings, new challenges, new uncertainties, and new stresses.

No doubt some of you, like Israel of old, are in the middle of situations that seem to lead toward destruction. Nothing about what you are enduring seems redeemable or redemptive. If so, this text is written for you.

Comprehensive Plans
The opening phrase of the promise, "For I know the plans I have for you," indicates something of the exhaustive scope of his plans for us.

First, we see that his plans are *known plans*. The word *I* is emphatic, suggesting that *"you* do not know the plans I have for you, and you may not think in your situation that anyone can, but *I know* the plans I have for you." Though the plans for our lives are unknown to us, they are perfectly known and hidden in him. Elsewhere the Scriptures tell us that, "As the heavens are higher than the earth, so are my ways higher than your ways and my thoughts than your thoughts" (Isaiah 55:9). And similarly, "Your path led through the sea, your way through the mighty waters, though your footprints were not seen" (Psalm 77:19). God's ways are inscrutable to us. But he knows exactly what he is doing.

At the beginning of the Babylonian Captivity, God knew what he was going to do for his people. And here, when everything seems confused and tangled, and we can make no sense out of it, God knows, and he says, "I know the plans I have for you."

His plans are so exhaustive, so comprehensive, that he knows in detail his plans for us.

But not only are his plans known, they are *eternal* plans, eternally conceived. There never was a time when he did not think of them. God's thoughts for his people are more ancient than Rome or Greece or the Himalayas, or Venus or Saturn, for that matter. "I have loved you with an everlasting love," says God. His plans are eternally exhaustive.

His plans are also *continual*. The Hebrew literally reads, "For I know the plans that *I am planning* for you." They are eternal plans, plans he is presently planning! He thinks about us so much that he actually numbers the hairs of our heads. The point is: there never has been and there never will be a thoughtless action of God's part toward me or you! Fate has never determined what has happened to us, God has. God is always thinking about us (Psalm 139:17).

Lastly, as to this matter of scope, his plans are *settled*. God's plans do not change as ours do. When you do not know your own mind, God does, and he knows his own mind concerning you. God knows all when we know nothing at all. His mind for us is made up.

Now assemble the facts we have drawn from this opening phrase, "I know the plans I have for you," as they instruct us about the exhaustive scope of his plans for us. His plans are *known* to him when everything is confusing to us. His plans are *eternal*, preceding time. His plans are *continual* as he is always thinking of what is best for us. And his plans are *settled*, solid, dependable.

What does this mean to us? Just this: *His plans are adequate.* Regardless of what we may think about what is facing us, regardless of how convoluted the situation may appear, his plans are adequate. In fact, they are exhaustively so. He knows what he is doing.

How He bends but never breaks
When our good He undertakes;
How He uses whom He chooses
And with every purpose fuses him;
By every act induces him

To try His splendor out—
God knows what He's about![1]

Good Plans

These elevated thoughts bring us to the very mountaintop of the promise, which is the *goodness* of God's plans for us. "I know the plans I have for you," declares the Lord, "plans for welfare and not for calamity." The profound depth of his goodness is perceived when we understand that the word for "welfare" is literally *shalom/peace*, a word that means not only the absence of trouble, but indicates completeness, soundness, welfare, well-being, and wholeness. Perhaps the best rendering is well-being or wholeness. The truth is, God's plans for everyone of us are for *shalom*, our well-being. There are no exceptions to this among God's children. You cannot be an exception— and never will be!

From this we understand that God can have no evil thoughts toward his own—no thoughts of calamity. He never has had an evil thought toward a child of his, and he never will. Theodore Laetsch, the Old Testament scholar, makes a most perceptive comment regarding this:

> His plans concerning his people are always thoughts of good, of blessing. Even if he is obliged to use the rod, it is the rod not of wrath, but the Father's rod of chastisement for their temporal and eternal welfare. There is not a single item of evil in his plans for his people, neither in their motive, nor in their conception, nor in their revelation, nor in their consummation.[2]

He's never had it, and never will!

This does not mean that God's servants are shielded from hardship or misery. What it does mean is that God's plans are never for evil in the believer's life, but with an eye to their well-being and wholeness—always! Even the apparent evil we suffer is toward our wholeness. Malcolm Muggeridge wrote in *A Twentieth Century Testimony*:

I can say with complete truthfulness that everything I have learned in my seventy-five years in this world, everything that has truly enhanced and enlightened my existence, has been through affliction and not through happiness, whether pursued or attained. In other words, if it ever were to be possible to eliminate affliction from our earthly existence by means of some drug or other medical mumbo-jumbo, as Aldous Huxley envisaged in *Brave New World*, the result would not be to make life delectable, but to make it too banal and trivial to be endurable.[3]

By his own witness, Malcolm Muggeridge's *shalom*, his wholeness, his well-being, is due to the difficulties he has faced. This is a life-changing revelation if taken to heart.

My own experience is that, through all of life, God has done nothing to me but good. He has afflicted me, yes! But he has never done me evil. Even when I lost my father as a four-year-old, even when disappointed and hurt by close friends, even in difficulties in child-rearing, *even in professional failures.* Truly, if I had come to College Church and not lasted six months, his goodness toward me would not have altered, nor would his "plans for welfare and not for calamity."

In Joseph Bayly's final column in *Eternity* magazine, a column he authored for over twenty years, Joe shared about his family. He said, "Since I've shared the severity of God with my readers" (speaking of the deaths of three of his children), "I want to share the goodness of God in this final column." And then he recounted God's grace in the lives of each of his four living children: Deborah, Timothy, David, and Nathan. And what is especially significant in relation to the truth of the text we are expounding are his final words:

Mary Lou and I are aware that all this represents the grace of God, but also that for ourselves and our children the road hasn't ended. Yet we know that both by his severity and by his goodness God has shown consistent faithfulness. God is good. He is worthy of all trust and all glory. Amen.[4]

And to that, what can we say, but "Amen!"? His plans are good "for welfare and not for calamity."

Optimistic Plans

Comprehensive, good plans bring optimism, and that is what is in the final line of his plans for us: "To give you a future and a hope." God's word to me through Jeremiah, and my friend Bob Noles, was that I had a future and I had reason to be hopeful.

Hope is the opposite of despair. It is intrinsically optimistic. I am to have an optimistic hope in *this life,* come what may. I am also to have a great hope in the life *beyond this life.*

In eternity, everything will come into focus. We will see it all! Think what will happen to our perspective during the first five minutes of heaven. Imagine what will happen to our perspective the first day, and the first ten thousand years! Brothers and sisters, if we could see God's plan for *shalom* in history and beyond, we would find ourselves like Peter even rejoicing in the trials of this life (1 Peter 4:12-13).

Fellow ministers, some of you may be in deep trouble right now. Life may seem to be falling apart. But take heart. Imbibe this promise's optimism—that you have a "future and a hope."

The Only Condition

Seeing that the Lord's plans for us are *comprehensive* and *good* and *optimistic,* we will naturally ask if there are any qualifications we must meet. The answer is that while the truth of these promises apply to all of God's people, there is a condition necessary to consciously *experience* its reality.

Biblical scholars agree that the condition is given in the immediately following context of Jeremiah 29:12-13.[5]

It is to *seek him with all our hearts.* "Then you will call upon me and come and pray to me, and I will listen to you. You will seek me and find me when you seek me with all your heart." There must be a God-focused obsession in our lives if we are to fully experience the benefit of his promise.

David put this obsession into classic wording in Psalm 42: "As the deer pants for streams of water, so my soul pants for you, O God. My soul thirsts for God, for the living God." And again in Psalm 63: "O God, you are my God, earnestly I seek you; my soul thirsts for you, my body longs for you, in a dry and weary land where there is no water." To such seeking, God gives the full experience of his promise. Half-hearted seeking will not bring it. Infrequent seeking is inadequate. The reality of Jeremiah 29:11 is given to wholehearted seekers.

But to those with this passion, the promise of God is alive with:

■ Comprehensiveness—"For I know the plans I have for you."
■ Goodness—"Plans of welfare and not for destruction."
■ Optimism—"To give you a future and a hope."

Fellow ministers, "If then you have been raised up with Christ, keep seeking the things above, where Christ is, seated at the right hand of God. Set your mind on the things above, not on the things that are on earth" (Colossians 3:1-2, NASB).

T W E L V E

Encouragement from the Call

There have been times, after sharing the details of my call to the ministry, I have heard it glibly psychologized away. Typically, it has gone something like this: "Don't you think that your background accounts for your 'call'? You mentioned that your father died when you were four, and that you were led to Christ by your pastor, who took a father-like interest in you. It seems obvious that the unusually intense conviction with which you were called was the result of psychological identification." And so, my divine call to the ministry is reduced to an unrequited paternal need.

Very neat! But such psychologizing has never discouraged me in the least. It has only strengthened my certainty—because I am convinced that the sovereign God who called me also arranged the events of my life to enhance the conviction of my call. My call to the ministry was *real!* And I am convinced that God calls certain of his children to this special service. To be sure, my experience of the call is not normative for anyone else, for the experience of God's call is as varied as there are people; only the reality is the same. Some slowly grow into the realization of their call, others are smitten with it in mid-life, and still others, like G. Campbell Morgan, can trace it to earliest memories.

For me the call sprang from the logical force of Romans

12:1 on my young mind: If God calls us to total dedication as the only "reasonable service of worship," then the only logical course was to become a minister.[1] The Holy Spirit used this to seal the conviction that I was called—a conviction that remained sublimely relentless through the years. My life bears testimony to the reality of my early call.

Those who would deny or minimize the fact that God calls individual Christians to special service must not only discount the facts of human experience but the evidence of Scripture, which records the calls of Moses, Isaiah, Jeremiah, Paul, and the commissioning of the apostles.[2]

Today, it is fashionable in some circles to downplay the ministerial call. Some do this because they believe that the ministry is simply another profession like that of a lawyer or banker. They fail to realize that, while God calls his people to different walks of life, the ministry is uniquely exalted because it is a special call to the care and feeding of souls. Still others downplay the ministerial call to avoid building a gap between the clergy and laity, which consigns ministry to the professional clergy and relieves the laity of responsibility.

Nevertheless, the ministry is the highest of calls. We must never downplay or minimize it.

Dr. Will Houghton, one-time minister of Calvary Baptist Church in New York City and president of Moody Bible Institute, put it this way:

> The highest calling man can know is the call to the Christian ministry. While it is true that every Christian is commissioned to labor together with Christ, it is also true that he has chosen some to undertake special service for him in their day and generation.
>
> God has a plan for every life, and men can serve the Lord just as heartily and helpfully in the marketplace and banking house as in the pulpit, but blessed is the man who feels in his heart the urge to preach the gospel.

Your speaker makes this confession. He would rather be the pastor of the smallest Baptist church you know, even if considered a failure by his friends, than to occupy some high position in society and be considered a success. . . .

The preacher does not select his vocation. It is selected for him by the One who said, "You have not chosen me, but I have chosen you," and he is commissioned and sent forth in the power of the Person of whom it was said, "He gave some to be apostles, some prophets, some evangelists and some pastors and teachers."[3]

Will Houghton's testimony is consonant with that of God's servants past and present.

Alexander Whyte, the great preacher of Edinburgh, wrote to a Methodist pastor friend, "The angels around the throne envy you your great work. . . . Go on and grow in grace and power as a gospel preacher."[4]

William Cowper the hymn writer wrote similarly:

There stands the messenger of truth: there stands
The legate of the skies—His theme divine,
His office sacred, his credentials clear.
By him the violated law speaks out
Its thunders; and by him, in strains as sweet
As angels use, the Gospel whispers peace.[5]

Dr. Martyn Lloyd-Jones, whose ministry was so used of God in Westminster Chapel, London, left a promising medical career to enter the ministry. Sometimes people would admiringly refer to his self-denial in becoming a minister, but he would immediately repudiate the intended compliment saying: "I gave up nothing; I received everything. I count it the highest honor that God can confer on any man to call him to be a herald of the gospel."[6]

Ray Stedman, the contemporary Bible expositor, concurs in describing his own experience:

I became aware of a growing sense in my own life of the grandeur of preaching. Of what I have called the majesty of ministry . . . I have felt a deeply humbling conviction that I will never be given a greater honor than what has already been given to me, that I should preach the unsearchable riches of Christ.[7]

Fellow servants, to be called to the ministry is, indeed, a supreme honor. But, as such, it is not a reason for pride, but rather deep humility. We must never minimize our call but exult in its divine origin and sanctify it with a life of devotion.

Power in the Call

In respect to our task, God's call is more important than theological education. No thinking person will ever set education and spirituality in contrast or conflict. Spirituality does not mean ignorance; neither does education indicate spiritual growth. Moreover, any rational person will get as much education as he can. But having said this, it is God's call, not education, that makes the minister—as is attested by the fact that John Bunyan, C. H. Spurgeon, D. L. Moody, G. Campbell Morgan, A. W. Tozer, and Billy Graham, to name a few, did not have theological educations! They were called, and, of course, being called to minister, they became students of the Word and keen practitioners of their calling.

The practical point for us here is that when God calls one to the ministry, he gives the requisite gifts to fulfill that ministry. Furthermore, he very often calls those who obviously would not be able to fulfill their calling apart from his gifts. Is this not what Paul means when he says, "But we have this treasure in jars of clay to show that this all-surpassing power is from God and not from us" (2 Corinthians 4:7)? Earlier, Paul says, "Not that we are competent in ourselves to claim anything for ourselves, but our competence comes from God. He has made us competent as ministers of a new covenant—not of the letter but of the Spirit; for the letter kills, but the Spirit gives life" (2 Corinthians 3:5-6).

The call of God means power for service! And one of the abiding glories of the gospel ministry is that our weakness is the occasion for his power—our shyness for his boldness, our inarticulateness for his articulation, our unimaginativeness for his creativity, our ignorance for his instruction, our dullness for his intelligence! *Your call means that you have power to fulfill it!* "The one who calls you is faithful and he will do it" (1 Thessalonians 5:24).

The Classic Call

The classic text for the call of God is Isaiah 6:1-13, which records the stupendous call and response of the prophet Isaiah. Few of God's servants, except perhaps Moses and Paul, have experienced anything approaching it. Nevertheless, there is a sense in which all who have responded to God's call will naturally relate to its classic elements—because these elements (in less spectacular form!) are common to the experience of all who have obeyed God's call to minister.

A vision of God's holiness. As Isaiah mourned the empty throne of Israel, he was suddenly caught up in a vision of the sovereign Lord majestically enthroned above him with the train of his robe carpeting the temple floor. Above the Lord, burning seraphim hovered, beating the air with one set of wings while covering their faces and feet with their remaining pinions in humble recognition that they were in the presence of perfect holiness. As Isaiah watched, he heard them chant repeatedly to one another, "Holy, holy, holy, is the Lord Almighty; the whole earth is full of his glory" (Isaiah 6:3). And with that the foundations of the temple began to sway and the smoke of God's presence filled the sanctuary as the glowing seraphim continued their chant.

Isaiah was stricken, overwhelmed with the absolute holiness of God! This experience became a permanent part of his psyche and was fundamental to his call. Isaiah saw that God is transcendently separate—other. He saw, too, that his purity is beyond human reach. This massive vision fostered the understanding that such a God demanded everything from him and that the demand began with his heart.

It is the same with us. Ultimately, our call to ministry rests upon our vision of God. A great God like this must be served. The greater our vision, the more compelling the call becomes.

A vision of our unholiness. A clear vision of God brings a clear vision of self, and that is traumatic: "'Woe to me,' I cried. 'I am ruined! For I am a man of unclean lips, and I live among a people of unclean lips, and my eyes have seen the King, the Lord Almighty'" (Isaiah 6:5). "Woe to me" is a cry of agony and mourning. Isaiah experienced immense moral anguish as he saw his sin. Wave upon wave of guilt washed over him.

Though he could not know it, he was in the way of blessing. The coming Messiah gave it perfect expression: "Blessed are those who mourn, for they will be comforted" (Matthew 5:4). We could well say, "Blessed are those who mourn over their sins and the sins of others, for they will be comforted."

Isaiah was about to be comforted with forgiveness, and it would become further ground for his call.

Forgiveness of sin. Isaiah describes it this way: "Then one of the seraphs flew to me with a live coal in his hand, which he had taken with tongs from the altar. With it he touched my mouth and said, 'See, this has touched your lips; your guilt is taken away and your sin atoned for.'" What relief, what joy, what gratitude coursed through

Isaiah's soul! And this became the immediate impulse for his saying yes to God's call when it came. It is the same for anyone who has ever obeyed God's call. It was the same for me and the same for you.

Think back, fellow servant, to the springtime of your call, and you will see that at the root of it is gratitude for his forgiveness. The logic is universal:

> *Love so amazing, so divine*
> *Demands my life, my soul, my all!*

Obedience. We need only glance at Isaiah's response to see how eager his obedience was: "Then I heard the voice of the Lord saying, 'Whom shall I send? And who will go for us?' And I said, 'Here am I. Send me!'"

We can all relate to Isaiah's classic call because its elements are common to the called. We find strength in refreshing ourselves to its elements: (1) a massive vision of God and his holiness, (2) a vision of our sinfulness, (3) the experience of forgiveness, and (4) obedience to the divine call. It is an honored progression. How privileged we have been to stand in it and say yes!

Living the Call

Every morning we ought to thank God for the privilege of being called and allowed to serve. It is as Phillips Brooks said in his famous Yale Lectures:

> I always remember one special afternoon, years ago, when the light faded from the room where I was preaching, and the faces melted together into a unit as of one impressive pleading man, and I felt them listening when I could hardly see them; I remember this accidental day as one of the times when the sense of the privilege of having to do with people as their preacher came out almost overpoweringly.[8]

Oh, for more servants of God who are overcome by the power of the call! Oh, for more ministers of the Word who treasure the privilege of presenting the Truth to the pleading men and women of the world!

THIRTEEN

Encouragement for the Ordinary

There have been times when I have been preaching and have felt as though I were standing apart from myself observing someone else speak. It has sometimes happened as I have become aware of an unnatural silence. The ever-present coughing ceases and the pews stop creaking, bringing an almost physical silence to the sanctuary—through which my words sail like arrows. I experience a heightened eloquence. An increased articulateness invades my speech so that the cadence and volume of my voice intensify the truth I am preaching. Though I know that I am speaking, I have thought at these times, "What is going on here? Is this me?" And then seeing it for what it is, my heart cries, "Lord, help me!"

What a dazzling experience! But as wondrous as it is, those who preach affirm that it is not unique. Thousands of preachers have like experiences, even greater ones. But what makes it so amazing to me is the fact that during the early years of my preaching there was little to indicate that I would ever experience this.

Though I had the temerity to attempt to "preach" when I was just sixteen years old, it was a painful experience for both me and my hearers because of my extreme self-conscious discomfort. And though I made other attempts during the following years and eagerly sought leadership positions in church and at school, public speaking remained very painful. I found I could not even make announcements unless I wrote them out and studied them well beforehand. Even after marriage, when I got up in front of a small group, my cheek would twitch uncontrollably and my face would sometimes grow deep red. So painful was speaking for me that Barbara would arrange to sit outside my peripheral vision so as not to distract me.

Yet few in my congregation today would suspect that I have ever been anything but a natural speaker. Some probably even think that I am in the ministry simply because I pursued my natural strength of public speaking. Not so! Rather, it never ceases to amaze me that I am able to stand and preach in the pulpit of any church. And at those times when the sanctuary assumes that telltale hush, I feel like pinching myself.

What is the point of my experience? Simply this: one of the supreme glories of the gospel ministry is that our weakness is the opportunity for his power—*our ordinariness for his extraordinariness*. It is a glory that I hold close to my heart, and with which I daily, sometimes hourly, refresh myself. It is a truth that has kept me going in the ministry. And this is why, apart from the Scriptures themselves, my most treasured quotation is the following, from Oswald Chambers:

> God can achieve his purpose either through the absence of human power and resources, or the abandonment of reliance on them. All through history God has chosen and used nobodies, because their unusual dependence on him made possible the unique display of his power and grace. He chose and used somebodies only when they renounced dependence on their natural abilities and resources.[1]

I cherish Chamber's beautiful expression not only because it capsulizes my experience but because it has been consistently confirmed by the history of the church, and is, as we shall see, powerfully verified by Scripture.

Chambers' words ought to be vastly encouraging to most of us because the majority of us are ordinary. As the saying goes, "God must have liked ordinary people because he made so many of them!" Yet, at the same time, his words should also be of encouragement to those who are unusually gifted, because even the most gifted do not have within themselves the abilities to succeed in God's calling. There is encouragement here for all, whether ordinary or extraordinary.

Ordinary Andrew

The Holy Spirit has gone to extensive length to make it clear in the Scriptures, both by human example and explicit statement, that God uses ordinary people. The most celebrated example is the Apostle Andrew, who is universally regarded as an average man. We'll call him "Ordinary Andrew." Though Andrew was the first of the Twelve to follow Jesus and thus bear the title *Protokletos,* "first-called," he did not become a prominent apostle. Though first in order, and brother to Simon Peter, he was not included in the inner circle of Peter, James, and John.

It is revealing to note that Andrew was regularly identified as the brother of Simon Peter. But Peter was never identified as the brother of Andrew! Everyone knew Peter. But Andrew? "Oh, you know who he is. He's the one who's always with Peter, the tagalong. Peter's brother." Andrew wrote no epistles, no miracles are recorded of him, and he was not an eloquent preacher like his brother. Ordinary Andrew was rarely, if at all, in the foreground, and definitely not regarded as a leader!

Nevertheless, he was so mightily used by God that today his name has first place in evangelism and missions. Years ago when the Billy Graham Evangelistic Association was looking for a title to encourage others to bring their friends to hear the gospel, they chose "Operation Andrew" because Andrew became the first evangelist when he brought his brother Peter to Christ (John 12:20-22). Tradition records that Ordinary Andrew became the patron saint of no less than three cultures: Eusebius says that he was the first missionary to go north of the Black Sea, and so the Russians claim him as their saint. Another tradition makes him the patron saint of Greece, for it says that he was martyred there on a X-shaped cross, where he hung for three days praying for his enemies. Finally, the white St. Andrew's Cross on a sky-blue background is the standard of Scotland. Tradition has it that after a monk brought Andrew's relics to Scotland, the Scots were led into battle by an X-shaped cross floating in the sky.[2] Why, apart from supposed historical precedent, do three nations claim Andrew? Because in the gospels, Andrew's name means caring evangelism. Ordinary Andrew's simple usefulness in bringing others to Christ has made his name one of winsome beauty, and whole nations compete to claim him for their own.

May the lesson not be wasted on us—*God uses ordinary people to do extraordinary work.* To be sure, we found several beautiful qualities in Andrew's life. Andrew thought of others first (John 1:40-42); Andrew was optimistic about what Christ could do with very little (John 6:5-9); and Andrew believed that Jesus was for everyone (John 12:20-22). But at the root of these virtues was his ordinariness. His ordinariness naturally made him aware of his human inadequacy, which, in turn, fostered his dependence upon God, making him extraordinarily useful to God and man.

The Glory of the Ordinary

Paul's writings powerfully substantiate that man's ordinariness, even his weakness, provides ready ground for God's extraordinary power. In discussing his own apostolic ministry, Paul made this unforgettable observation: "But we have this treasure in jars of clay to show that this all-surpassing power is from God and not from us" (2 Corinthians 4:7). Paul summarized the secret of his ministry by referring to the ancient custom of hiding priceless treasure in common earthen, clay pots beneath the earth. The "treasure" was the gospel, and the "jars of clay," a penetrating metaphor for frail humanity. Thus the glorious gospel is committed to common, frail human beings—so that the immensity of the power may be seen as God's and not man's! Clearly then, an awareness of one's weakness, one's ordinariness, can be an asset in the gospel ministry, for such an awareness may more easily depend upon the power of God. Conversely, it can be a disadvantage to be extraordinarily gifted, because one can then be tempted to rely upon natural gifts to achieve supernatural ends.

There have been many preachers who, because they were so naturally gifted, never came to be the preachers they could have been. Their reliance upon their natural eloquence fostered a regrettable independence from God in respect to prayer and preparation. This is not to say, however, that the extraordinarily gifted are intrinsically disadvantaged, for the fact is, even the most extraordinary (like Paul!) are at best "jars of clay." The disadvantage for the extraordinary is that they may find it more difficult to see themselves for what they really are.

Being an ordinary Andrew is not a disadvantage in serving God. It can even serve as the basis for profound dependence upon him and yield extraordinary usefulness in ministry.

This was Gideon's experience when he delivered his people from the Midianites. In fact when the call came to him, he objected because of his *ordinariness*. "'But Lord,' Gideon asked, 'how can I save Israel? My clan is the weakest in Manasseh, and I am the least in my family'" (Judges 6:15). This was the kind of man God could use. Gideon would have to depend on the Lord. And depend he did!

Since the Midianite host was "as numerous as the locusts" Gideon naturally recruited a vast army of some 32,000 so he could match them strength for strength. It was a sane and responsible action. It would have been crazy to do otherwise. But the Lord had other ideas: "The

Lord said to Gideon, 'You have too many men for me to deliver Midian into their hands. In order that Israel may not boast against me that her own strength has saved her . . .'" (Judges 7:2). Instead of allowing Gideon to increase the army, the Lord ordered a ritual divestment of power! First, all who were afraid were allowed to go home, reducing the army by 22,000. Then the 10,000 who remained were ordered to drink water from the river. Only the 300 who drank from their hands were retained! From ground level it was ritual insanity—especially when the 300 went forth to battle armed only with trumpets and pitchers.

But it was during this conscious renunciation of natural power—this profound dependence upon God—that God was pleased to work. And humble Gideon led his people to a mighty victory. Human weakness became the occasion for God's power.

The full-blown expression of this principle is found in 2 Corinthians 12:9-10 where Paul says: "But he said to me, 'My grace is sufficient for you, for my power is made perfect in weakness.' Therefore I will boast all the more gladly about my weaknesses, so that Christ's power may rest on me. That is why, for Christ's sake, I delight in weaknesses. . . . For when I am weak, then I am strong."

That *weakness brings strength* is one of the great paradoxes of Christian experience! G. K. Chesterton once described a paradox as "truth standing on its head crying for attention." And that is certainly what we have here. Tragically, however, much of professing Christianity appears to have ignored it. Strength in the church goes to the strong, the wealthy, the sleek, the privileged. Christ's truth desperately needs attention.

Those of us in ministry especially need to embrace this paradox. For the men and women God has used have always lived with the reality that they are merely clay. When they saw Jesus Christ, they became unconscious of all they used to call their wisdom and strength. And rather than focus on their weakness, they made it their business to open wide for all his treasure. From this flowed the surpassing greatness of his power. Ordinary Andrews became vehicles for the extraordinary. There is glory in the ordinary!

Extraordinary Fullness

We can understand how ordinariness can invite the extraordinary in yet another way. It is found in the staggering pronouncement of Colossians 2:9-10: "For in Christ all the fullness of the Deity lives in bodily form, and you have been given fullness in Christ." There is a beautiful play on words here that heightens the force of the assertion: The *fullness* of deity dwells in Christ, and we are made *full* in him! How can this be? We can understand how the fullness can be in Christ.[3] But in what sense can his fullness dwell in us puny, finite creatures?

The answer can be best understood by way of illustration. During the writing of this book, Barbara and I stood on the shore of the vast Pacific Ocean—two finite dots alongside a seemingly infinite expanse. And as we stood there, we reflected that if I were to take a pint jar and allow the ocean to rush into it, in an instant my pint would be filled with fullness of the Pacific. But I could never put the fullness of the Pacific Ocean into my jar! Thinking of Christ, we realized that because he is infinite, he is greater than the Pacific, and so he can hold all the fullness of deity. And whenever one of us finite creatures dips the tiny vessel of our life into him we instantly become full of his fullness.

From the perspective of our humanity, the capacity of our containers are of greatest importance. Our souls are elastic, so to speak. And there are no limits to possible capacity. We can always open to hold more and more of his fullness. The walls can always stretch further; the roof can always rise higher; the floor can always hold more. The more we receive of his fullness, the more we *can* receive!

And this is where being Ordinary Andrews can serve as a definite advantage. Ordinary people can more readily realize their need, and open wide their lives for Christ's fullness; whereas the unusually gifted may be lulled by their adequacy to feel no need.

Simply put, being ordinary can open us wide to the ocean of Christ's fullness, and yield greater joy and power and service.

Extraordinary Perspective

In the opening chapters of 1 Corinthians, in which Paul subjects the ministry of the gospel to penetrating analysis, he urges a radical perspective for those who would follow Christ. He says: "Brothers, think of what you were when you were called. Not many of you were wise by human standards; not many were influential; not many were of noble birth. But God chose the foolish things of the world to shame the wise; God chose the weak things of the world to shame the strong. He chose the lowly things of the world and the despised things . . . so that no one may boast before him. . . . Therefore, as it is written, 'Let him who boasts boast in the Lord'" (1 Corinthians 1:26-29, 31).

Once again we see that God chooses to use ordinary people to serve him! He chooses them so there will be no mistake where the power comes from and so human boasting will be excluded. It is just as Chambers so eloquently said, "All through history God has chosen and used nobodies, because their unusual dependence on him made possible the unique display of his power and grace." Moreover, "He chose and used somebodies only when they renounced their dependence on their natural abilities and resources." This is, indeed, one of the great mysteries and glories of the gospel ministry!

For those of us who have been called to serve Christ, this truth demands that we do at least three things. First, we must thank God for our ordinariness, even our weaknesses. This is the one thing many have never done, because it goes against our natural dispositions. More often our ordinariness has been the cause for resentment rather than appreciation, just as when, by foolishly comparing myself with others, I angrily concluded that God had called me to do something he had not equipped me to do. Nevertheless, though we may find it difficult, even unnatural, to thank God for our ordinariness, it is the one thing we must do! When we do this, it liberates us from the tyranny of comparison with others and opens our lives to receive the fullness of God's power. Why not do it now? Why not list your areas of ordinariness and then reverently, from the bottom of your heart, thank God for them one by one? You can do it. Will you?

The second thing we must do is thank God for whatever extraordinary gifts and strengths we may have. This is so much easier! No doubt this has been done by virtually all who have attempted to serve Christ. Extraordinary gifts must elicit ardent appreciation. But there is a further necessary step here that is not so common. We must divest ourselves of all reliance upon our natural strengths. Here, a ritual divestment is in order—taking each of our strengths, one by one, and emptying ourselves of all reliance upon them apart from Christ. This will make possible the unique outworking of his power in our lives.

The final thing we must do is thank God for our call to the ministry, for it is the ministry that fosters in us a profound awareness of our ordinariness and inadequacy. The demands of preaching, counseling, and leading constantly bring us to the end of ourselves and the beginning of his power. Each of us ought to celebrate our call to the ministry every day. We ought to thank God for being called to a life that expands our souls and maximizes our spiritual growth.

What is more, we ought to celebrate our ordinariness, for it is with the ordinary that God is so often pleased to do the extraordinary.

FOURTEEN

Encouragement from Fellow Workers

On an unforgettable Sunday morning in 1866, the great C. H. Spurgeon stunned his five thousand listeners when from the pulpit of London's Metropolitan Tabernacle he announced, "I am the subject of depressions of spirit so fearful that I hope none of you ever gets to such extremes of wretchedness as I go to." For some of his audience it was incomprehensible that the world's greatest preacher could know the valley of despair. Yet twenty-one years later in 1887 he said from the same pulpit, "Personally I have often passed through this dark valley."

John Henry Jowett, the brilliant pastor of Fifth Avenue Presbyterian in New York City, and later Westminster Chapel in London, wrote to a friend in 1920, "You seem to imagine I have no ups and downs but just a level and lofty stretch of spiritual attainment with unbroken joy and equanimity. By no means! I am often perfectly wretched and everything appears most murky."

G. F. Barbour, the biographer of Alexander Whyte, perhaps Scotland's greatest preacher since John Knox, said of Whyte, "Resolute as was Dr. Whyte's character, he had seasons of deep depression regarding the results of his work in the pulpit or among his people. . . ."[1]

Martin Luther was subject to such fits of darkness that he would secret himself away for days, and his family would remove all dangerous implements from the house for fear he would harm himself. In the midst of one of these times, his wife, Katherine, entered his room dressed in mourning. Startled, Luther asked who had died. She replied that no one had, but from the way he was acting, she thought God had died!

The truth is, godly believers sometimes get depressed! Those who have set their minds on "the things above, where Christ is seated at the right hand of God," have not been exempted from depression. Those who have gone for it all, who have scaled heights we may never attain, sometimes were subject to depression and despair—the "damp of hell" as John Donne called it. [2] Depression has been called the common cold of the mind, for sooner or later most people catch it. God's servants are not immune.

Ministerial depression actually has apostolic precedent in the experience of the Apostle Paul. He was a great apostle, but the ministry had gotten to him, and he was "depressed"—his word (2 Corinthians 7:6, NASB)! He was, as the Greek word suggests, lowly and downcast. But the beautiful thing for us here is that he does not attempt to hide it. In fact, he actually tells us the cause of his depression and what God did to heal him. And his answer, taken to heart, proves a great boon for those in Christian ministry.

The Anatomy of a Ministerial Depression

Paul is perfectly clear and succinct in 2 Corinthians 7: "For when we came into Macedonia, this body of ours had no rest, but we were harassed at every turn—conflicts on the outside, fears within." In just one sentence the apostle gives three reasons for his depression.

First, Paul was worn out. By saying, "For when we came into Macedonia, this body of ours had no rest," Paul reveals that he was physically exhausted. This is because of the incessant intrigues and plots on his life by both Jews and Gentiles of which Paul earlier spoke, "We do not want you to be uninformed, brothers, about the hardships we suffered in the province of Asia. We were under great pressure, far beyond our ability to endure, so that we despaired even of life" (2 Corinthians 1:8). Of this, the Princeton expositor Charles Hodge says that the picture here is of a wearied animal that sinks in despair beneath a burden beyond its own strength.[3] Recently, Paul had been so exhausted by the constant harassment and lack of rest that he felt he was going to die. He had difficulty picking himself up to continue. As a result the old warrior was worn out and depressed.

It is universally acknowledged that fatigue is a standard cause of depression; then it is universally forgotten! That exhaustion promotes depression was never more clearly modeled than by Elijah. There have been few prophets with more starch than Elijah. Few have ever displayed such resolve in the face of conflict as he did in facing the 450 prophets of Baal, taunting them to cry louder, and suggesting that Baal was on vacation or asleep (1 Kings 18:27). Here was a real man! He must have been in good shape, too, because after he defeated the prophets, he gathered up his robes and outran Ahab's chariot some eighteen miles to Jezreel.

What an astounding victory—and what a man! But then the most amazing thing happened; this same Elijah, who had just destroyed the 450 fake prophets, heard that Jezebel had threatened his life, succumbed to fear, fled into the wilderness, and in deep depression asked God to take his life (1 Kings 18:3-4). Why? Why after such a resounding victory? The obvious answer is that he was worn out. His "body had no rest," and the eighteen-mile "jog" hadn't helped either! That Elijah's depression was due largely to exhaustion is verified by the fact that he fell asleep, was awakened by an angel who fed him, fell asleep again, and again was awakened and fed (1 Kings 19:5-8).

Exhaustion can make a coward and a depressive out of just about anyone! I say this because Barbara and I have observed, both in the pastorate and on the mission field, a ministerial machismo which fancies that devotion to God exempts one from the physical rules that govern other mortals. The godly, it is supposed, somehow need less sleep, less food, less rest, and less recreation than the ungodly. True, God does give his servants extraordinary energy for emergencies and challenges, but over the long haul, the ministry is performed in bodies subject to the same laws as those of everyone else. Sometimes we get depressed, and we wonder why. Paul's explanation gives the answer. Our flesh has had no rest.

Second, Paul was pressured. Verse 5 continues, "But we were harassed at every turn—conflicts on the outside." Here "harassed" carries the idea of squeezed or pressured, and "conflicts" literally means fightings. He was pressured from all sides by people pressures. He could not escape. Every turn brought him face to face with pressures. Later, in answer to those who were challenging his apostolic credentials, Paul reticently listed the external hardships he had known for the gospel, intoning a terrible litany of abuses (11:23-30). Such was his pressured life. And we must note that with these pressures and fightings came the debilitating ache of rejection. Few pressures are more draining and depressing than estrangement and rejection.

Third, Paul feared. The same Paul who stood before kings and hostile crowds to proclaim Christ had "fears within." So we see that even the greatest have inner fears and anxieties. However, in Paul's case, we must discard any idea that he feared for his own life. We have too much evidence to the contrary to think that (Philippians 1:21-24; 2:17). His inner fears were for what might happen to his work, for he often spoke of this: "I *fear* for you, that somehow I have wasted my efforts on you" (Galatians 4:11); "For this reason, when I could stand it no longer, I sent to find out about your faith. I was *afraid* that in some way the tempter might have tempted you and our efforts might have been

146

useless" (1 Thessalonians 3:5); "I face daily the pressure of my concern for all the churches. Who is weak, and I do not feel weak? Who is led into sin, and I do not inwardly burn?" (2 Corinthians 11:28-29). These ministerial fears weighed heavily on Paul. He was always aware of some-one in one of the churches who was falling away. Ecclesi-astic conflicts were his daily fare, and he was constantly writing to calm the waters and set things straight.

Phillips Brooks, the peerless preacher and one-time Episcopal bishop of Boston, said:

> To be a true minister to men is always to accept new happiness and new distress. . . . The man who gives himself to other men can never be a wholly sad man; but no more can he be a man of unclouded gladness. To him shall come with every deeper consecration a before untasted joy, but in the same cup shall be mixed a sor-row that it was beyond his power to feel before.[4]

Put another way, Paul had a "heart problem"—an en-larged heart! The bigger the ministerial heart, the greater is the potential for the flesh having no rest—conflicts without—and fears within.

Paul was depressed. How would you help Paul? Send him a tract? Write him a closely reasoned letter reminding him of the theological realities? Probably not. After all, he *wrote* the theological realities.

The Titus Touch
The divine answer for Paul's depression was this, "But God, who comforts the downcast [depressed], comforted us by the coming of Titus" (2 Corinthians 7:6). Comfort came in a person named Titus.

Elisa, a poor woman, had just lost her son and was in the depths of grief. Her godly friend, Anna, joined her, and they knelt in prayer by the bedside. As they prayed, Anna suggested that Elisa ask God to lay his hand on her head. When Elisa made the request, Anna softly laid her hand on her head. "He's done it! Glory to God!" cried Elisa. Her friend coaxed her to tell about it, and Elisa replied, "There was a wonderful feeling that went down through me, and the hand was just like yours."

"The hand was mine," replied Anna gently, "but it was God's hand too." This was the touch of comfort and encouragement. Put another way, it was the "Titus Touch"—the hand of God.

This literally happened in my life. It had been an exhausting week. Things had not gone well—and I had had little time for study. I was depressed as I faced a mountain of undone administrative work and the prospect of preparing a sermon in the too little time that was left. As I prayed over my work, I was shamefully despairing. But as I opened the morning mail I read this:

> Dear Pastor Kent:
>   Thank you so very much for being our Pastor.
>   We love you and Barbara and your family. You are a special gift to us.
>   Thank you for caring for our souls, and contending with us against those lures and forces that would take us away from God's best.
>   Persist! Please don't give up on us.
>
> Have a pleasant, blessed Christmas,
> *Tedd*

As I finished the note I was energized. Though the work had not gone away, the burden lifted—and I went refreshed to a busy weekend of ministry. That is what someone who cares can do. We are down, and we cry to God. And help comes in the form of another like us—if there is one who is willing to be the hand and heart of God.

What did Titus say? "Paul, old friend, how are you? Oh, not so good, huh? You say you're depressed? Come on, Paul. You're an apostle! You can't do this. Here, let me read you a verse."

That's not what he did! The first thing Titus did was to put his arms around Paul and kiss him. That is the first thing Jewish friends did—always. Then Titus listened to Paul, empathized with his depression, participated in his hurt, and prayed with him.

What did Paul do? It is not in the text, but it is implicit. He revealed his ministerial depression to Titus. Paul was not hung up on the "good Christians don't have any problems" thinking. If he was, he would never have written 2 Corinthians. Paul bared his heart.

As to what Titus said to Paul, the text reveals that he affirmed Paul with the affirmations of others: "But God, who comforts the downcast, comforted us by the coming of Titus, and not only by his coming but also by the comfort you had given him. He told us about your longing for me, your deep sorrow, your ardent concern for me, so that my joy was greater than ever."

"Paul, they miss you. You see, there really are people who care whether you live or die. They long for you. They mourn over the difficulties they have caused you. They are zealous in their concern for you." Paul was elevated, and so he says, "My joy was greater than ever."

Oh, how God's servants need this ministry! Some years ago I read that Phillips Brooks kept a file of encouraging notes and letters for "rainy days," and during such times would pull them out and reread them. So I began my own file. I keep every encouraging letter I receive, and there are occasions that I read them again. But, even more, I began to write many more encouraging notes to others, especially to my colleagues in the ministry. The ministry of affirmation! It's something we must do.

The Healing Power of Friendship

Depression may be the common cold of human experience, but when you catch it, it is the damp of hell.[5] None of us is exempt just because we love God and have a high degree of consecration. The actual truth is, if we have ministering hearts, we are even more vulnerable to depression. Dedicated servants get tired bodies, they experience accelerated conflicts, sometimes they have fears within, and sometimes they get depressed.

Very often, God's plan for healing is by "the coming of Titus," the Titus Touch. As ministers of the gospel in the apostolic train, we all *need* Tituses, and we all need to *be* Tituses. To this end, there are several things we must do.

First, cultivate friendships. The longer I have lived, the more I have learned to value friendship. When young, though I certainly did not depreciate friendship, I thought that its development could wait for a less busy time in life. I had so much to do in preparation for ministry. But some years ago I saw that life does not slow down and that friendships are a major source of joy. Moreover, I realized that all relationships endure—some good and growing, some otherwise. So I learned to treasure relationships and build friendships. Among friendships, old ministerial friendships are particularly sweet by virtue of their commonality and natural exchange. Those who cultivate deep friendships are rich, whatever may be happening in the rest of life.

Second, be a friend. This, of course, means investing time, keeping a lively interest in others, encouraging others, corresponding, calling, and remembering. But it also means commitment, being willing to follow Christ's guidance in friendship, even if it means your own discomfort, so you can sometimes say, "That was mine, but it was God's too." Often when ministers get together, for example, at annual conferences, it is just the opposite. Though there are always many who are hurting, the upbeat expectations forbid Pauline honesty and vulnerability, and therefore inhibit the giving or receiving of a Titus Touch. We must resist this, sensitively looking for opportunities to get outside ourselves and encourage our comrades.

Third, allow someone to "Titus Touch" you. I recall some

seminary students expressing their frustration over trying to comfort a fellow student. He was in obvious depression, but whenever another would try to minister to him, he would reject him with angry words. Not Paul. He chose to receive the comfort Titus brought, even though Titus was the disciple! It is a humbling thing for the minister to receive comfort, but when he does it is beautiful.

Fellow ministers, cultivate friendships, be a friend, allow others to be a friend to you. Spread the wealth of the Titus Touch.

FIFTEEN

Encouragement from Reward

When Barbara and I moved to Wheaton, we had the privilege of developing a close friendship with Joe and Mary Lou Bayly. For years Joe had been president of a Christian publishing company as well as a well-known columnist in *Eternity* magazine. In addition to his heavy schedule of writing and speaking, Joe team-taught an adult Sunday school class at College Church for many years.

In 1976 Joseph Bayly's remarkable little book *Heaven* was published, and it began with an account of his reflections before a recent surgery:

> *It's six-thirty on a Tuesday morning.*
> *Here I am, waiting.*
>
> *Waiting to be wheeled into*
> *an operating room at Mayo Clinic's*
> *Methodist Hospital. . . .*
>
> *I wait for the merciful anesthesia,*
> *then the surgeon, and then . . .*
> *to come back to consciousness in the*
> *room where dear Mary Lou, my*
> *wife of thirty-two winters—*
> *and summers—also waits.*
>
> *Or to come back to consciousness in*
> *the presence of my Lord Christ.*[1]

A decade later, in the summer of 1986, Joe Bayly once again waited at the Mayo Clinic Hospital in Rochester. And this time, after ten more winters and summers with his beloved wife and family, he awoke in the presence of the Lord Christ in glory—where he began the adventure of his eternal reward. In an instant, everything his poet's imagination ever dreamed of came true!

In this life Joe Bayly had reason to think much about heaven because three of his sons preceded him while still in their youth—Danny at age four, Johnny as an infant, and Joe at eighteen. Because of this, his writings, rich with experience and theological reflection, have been a vast help to thousands. Through his long ministry to the bereaved, Joe realized that many have trouble believing in heaven or, at least, imagining it. So in his classic *The Last Thing We Talk About* he penned this exquisite parable, which is now his experience. He wrote:

> I cannot prove the existence of heaven.
>
> I accept its reality by faith, on the authority of Jesus Christ: "In my Father's house are many mansions; if it were not so, I would have told you. I go to prepare a place for you."
>
> For that matter, if I were a twin in the womb, I doubt that I could prove the existence of earth to my mate. He would probably object that the idea of an earth beyond the womb was ridiculous, that the womb was the only earth we'd ever know.
>
> If I tried to explain that earthlings live in a greatly expanded environment and breathe air, he would only be skeptical. After all, a fetus lives in water; who could imagine its being able to live in a universe of air? To him such a transition would seem impossible.
>
> It would take birth to prove the earth's existence to a fetus. A little pain, a dark tunnel, a gasp of air—and then the world outside! Green grass, laps, lakes, the ocean, horses (could a fetus imagine a horse?), rain-

bows, walking, running, surfing, ice-skating. With enough room that you don't have to shove, and a universe beyond.[2]

In that sublime second when Joe Bayly, himself, emerged from the dark tunnel of this life, metaphor became reality. He saw that the earth is indeed a womb when compared with the bounding life beyond; and the implications of his being in Christ burst over him in overflowing fullness. Upon seeing Christ, he was instantly transformed into his likeness, just as the Scriptures promise: "Dear friends, now we are children of God, and what we will be has not yet been made known. But we know that when he appears, we shall be like him, for we shall see him as he is" (1 John 3:2). And not only did he see Christ, he also saw the faces of his departed sons. In his book *Heaven* he asked the question:

> "Can I see my sons who died a
> few years ago? And my parents,
> Mary Lou's parents? My brother?"
>
> "Of course you'll see them.
> All of them trusted me on earth."[3]

Now enjoying the leisure of eternity, he is making up for "lost time" with his boys. Joe Bayly knows the arms of Christ, the arms of his family, and the arms of the body of Christ—the church he so loved and served. What must it be like? Can we imagine his ecstasy? Only partially, for it exceeds even Joe Bayly's remarkable imagination!

Oh, to hear what he has to say now! Of course it would be unfair to call him back from his reward, even for a moment. But suppose we could. Suppose he was allowed to materialize for a few moments with his favorite fountain pen in hand (Joe always wrote with a fountain pen), and was given the space on these pages to encourage Christ's servants. What would he say?

Heaven's Reality

It is very likely that Joe would begin by repeating what he said over and over again in his life and writings—that *heaven is real!* Perhaps he would remind us that the Scriptures say, "We fix our eyes not on what is seen, but on what is unseen. For what is seen is temporary, but what is unseen is eternal" (2 Corinthians 4:18), and that, in this way of thinking, he is more *real* than you or I.

Joe, despite his enviable gifts of expression, would have difficulty explaining the reality of his existence. "Can you imagine the difficulty," he once wrote, "of describing a pineapple to an Eskimo in the Arctic tundra? 'Sweet and juicy blubber' is about as close as you can come. Or how could you describe ice to a desert tribe? How could I tell earth people of heaven?"[4] Joe would, indeed, have difficulty. He would employ some new metaphors and similes. Our spiritual intelligence would be taxed. And we would miss much, but the general message would be clear.

He would tell us that heaven is a *place*, not just a spiritual state. He would remind us that when Jesus said, "I am going there to prepare a place for you" (John 14:2), he meant it. He would affirm that he understood something of it in this life through the work of the Holy Spirit, just as it is written: "'No eye has seen, no ear has heard, no mind has conceived what God has prepared for those who love him'—but God has revealed it to us by his Spirit" (1 Corinthians 2:9-10).[5]

His creative mind saw something of it by the revelation of the Holy Spirit, and that is why he wrote so powerfully of heaven. But now he literally has new eyes and ears. In heaven he is seeing a spectrum of colors impossible for the human eye and dazzling beauties beyond description. His human ears now hear sounds and tones beyond the capability of the earthbound. Heaven is a symphony of shapes and colors and textures and sounds designed and orchestrated by the hand of Christ. Furthermore, Joe's body is freed from the wearisome limitations of the earth, and he is at liberty to converse and sing and worship without physical discomfort and the strictures of time. Heaven is real, his place is real, he is real—and the reality is stupendous. Earth's realities were but shadows in comparison.

Heaven's Happiness

Joe Bayly quoted the psalmist, assuring us that heaven is a place of total happiness: "In Thy presence is fullness of joy, at Thy right hand there are pleasures for evermore."[6] How much more would he urge this reality upon us now!

Though Joe was an upbeat person who loved to laugh and make others laugh, he knew more than his share of sorrowful losses in this life. Neither was he a stranger to the heartache that comes from caring about others. But when he saw the face of Christ, the memory of the hard things gave way to unbroken, eternal bliss, as every tear was wiped away by the hand of Christ! "He will wipe away every tear from their eyes. There will be no more death or mourning or crying or pain, for the old order of things has passed away" (Revelation 21:4). The immense glory of heaven dissolved all earthly pain and replaced it with unending joy.

This brings us to the grand realization of the truth in 2 Corinthians 4:17 (NASB): "Momentary, light affliction is producing for us an eternal weight of glory far beyond all comparisons" ("in excess and to excess";[7] "out of all proportion").[8] So massive is the glory that life's troubles, however great and protracted they may be, are "light" in comparison.

We need to believe this. We need to have such an assurance of the glory and happiness to come that we can say with Paul, "For I consider that our present sufferings are not worth comparing with the glory that will be revealed in us" (Romans 8:18). Such a conviction of heaven's happiness held close will not fail to encourage us to keep on through the "thick and thin" of ministerial life.

Heaven's Reward

If Joe's pen were writing this, he would further say that we ministers must take seriously the biblical doctrine of rewards and that we must not be put off by those who say that to desire heavenly rewards is mercenary. Christ himself often used rewards as an incentive for service, and Scripture approves of seeking "glory, honor and immortality" (Romans 2:7). Moreover, as C. S. Lewis so rightly said:

> We must not be troubled by unbelievers when they say that this promise of rewards makes the Christian's life a mercenary affair. There are different kinds of reward. There is the reward which has no natural connection with things you do to earn it, and is quite foreign to the desires that ought to accompany those things. Money is not the natural reward of love; that is why we call a man mercenary if he marries a woman for the sake of her money. But marriage is the proper reward for a real lover, and he is not mercenary for desiring it.[9]

Because the church is the bride of Christ, it is only proper that she long for the Marriage Feast and the rewards of Christ, her lover. Anything less is unnatural. Indeed, not to desire spiritual reward is a sinful neglect of spiritual reality.

The Bible is clear that while believers will *not* stand in judgment for their sin because this is forever past for those in Christ (Romans 5:1), and salvation is a free gift (Ephesians 2:9-10), *the works of believers, nevertheless, will be judged:* "For we must all appear before the judgment seat of Christ" (2 Corinthians 5:10); "So then, each of us will give an account of himself to God" (Romans 14:12). The picture the Bible gives of this judgment is one of individual believers presenting their lives' works to Christ in the form of buildings. The eternal foundation of each building is Christ, but the structures vary. Some are made totally of wood, hay, and straw; others are of gold, silver, and precious stones; still others are composite structures of all the elements in individual proportions. As the architecture of each life is presented, it is publicly subjected to the revealing torch of Christ's judgment, and with the flames comes the moment of truth: "If any man builds on this foundation using gold, silver, costly stones, wood, hay or straw, his work will be shown for what it is, because the Day will bring it to light. It will be revealed with fire, and the fire will test the quality of each man's work. If what he has built survives, he will receive his reward. If it is burned up, he will suffer loss; he himself will be saved, but only as one escaping through the flames" (1 Corinthians 3:12-15).

There are degrees of reward for God's children. Some just barely get in the door, but nevertheless into heaven and eternal bliss because their faith is founded upon Christ, though their works are negligible. Others find that their soul's architecture has become the basis for even more reward measured out by the hand of Christ!

Today, because Joe Bayly lives with the full revelation of this truth, he would implore us to understand that God does not judge as man judges. To be sure, many of the noted Christians of church history and of this present age received the greatest rewards. But there were also some startling omissions. Some of those to whom everyone looked for leadership and whose names were common to everyone's lips, were saved "as though by fire." On the other hand, there were a disproportionate number of unknown believers who received eternal rewards equal to, and even above, the celebrated saints of human record. The Lord's dictum that "Indeed there are those who are last who will be first, and first who will be last" (Luke 13:30) is eternally true! The size and fame of one's work and personal prestige and importance mean nothing to Christ. The hearts that produce the architecture are the ones that endure—gold, silver, and precious stones.

Seeing that the Bible teaches that there are degrees of heavenly reward for believers, we naturally ask, how? Since all of God's children are going to see the face of

Christ, be transformed into his image, and experience eternal bliss, how can there be degrees of reward? How is a perfect reward to be improved upon? Here we cannot know for sure because the Scriptures are only suggestive. But perhaps one's developed capacity for enjoyment of heaven is part of the answer. We all know that the enjoyment of art or music is proportionate to one's cultivated ability. For example, two people can walk the halls of the Louvre and have quite opposite experiences; one experiences absolute boredom, the other ecstasy. The reason? One has previously developed an aesthetic sense and the other has not. Of course, in heaven, both would be in ecstasy, but possibly the one whose life's work was gold, silver, and precious stone would experience greater ecstasy. Perhaps there is an earth-developed architecture of soul that makes heaven even more wonderful. But whatever the case may be, there certainly will be degrees of rewards if we are to believe the Holy Scriptures.

There awaits for *all* believers an eternal "weight of glory" far beyond all comparison, because "when Christ, who is your life, appears, then you also will appear with him in glory" (Colossians 3:4). That glory will consist of honor with him, and from him. He will place crowns upon his childrens' heads to honor their individual services.[10] They will thrill to the divine benediction "well done, good and faithful servant" (Matthew 25:21). He will reward their service with greater service.[11] All will live in eternal awareness of his smile—and that glory will be reward enough in itself.

But there is even more, for when his children are revealed with him in glory, they will also share in his glorious splendor. The Bible says that believers will shine like the sun (Matthew 13:43), and that they will be given the Morning Star (Revelation 2:28; 22:16). Believers will *participate* in the splendor, not merely witness it. So Christ's faithful servants are destined to become beings of surpassing glory!

What are we to make of this staggering revelation? Simply this: It is not wrong to desire the reward of heaven, nor to labor with an eye to the splendor. Rather, it is evidence of spiritual health. In fact, the more intense the desire and commitment, the greater one's spiritual health, for it means that one not only understands, but *believes* what the Bible says about eternal rewards.

God will be no one's debtor. Those who serve him from the heart will receive rewards that far exceed whatever sacrifice was required. You may be laboring in humble anonymity or your name may be a household word; you may be ministering to a handful or to thousands; you may be seeing small or great results in your ministry; you may be in the valley of trial or on the mountaintop; but whatever your present situation, God sees everything and will reward you with lavish equity. In fact, if we could know for a moment what Joe Bayly is now experiencing—the reality, the *fact* of Christ, the happiness, the fellowship, the rewards, the "weight of glory"—we would find ourselves content to serve the Lord wherever we are and with all that we have!

Heaven's Demands

These realities, the realities of eternity, make important demands of us. And very prominent among them is that we treasure our time on earth for serving God, just as Joe Bayly encouraged in his *Psalm about the Shortness of Life*.

I said
O Lord
let me end the work
You gave me to do.
So much
must yet be done
before the dark
so little time
remains

before I'm home.
You are eternal
God
a thousand years to You
is but a passing day.
You scatter ages
I hoard my hours.
Please understand
my need for time
to do Your will
complete my job.
I understand
He said
I do
I only had
three years
of days
and I was through. [12]

The spiritual mathematics are inescapable, for compared with eternity our lives are truly vapors (James 4:14); yet what we do here in the fleeting moments of our existence has unending consequences for the world and our own souls. We must take advantage of the mathematics while we can, using our passing moments to bring eternal life to lost souls and to glorify God. We must call upon Christ, who knew the strictures of time, to make our lives count. In so doing our souls will naturally begin to assume an architecture pleasing to him.

The other demand the reality of heaven makes upon us is that we fix our minds on the eternal. Once more, the voice of Joe Bayly would call us to this. In his very last sermon preached before his home church, he urged serious commitment to holy living through the focus on eternal reality, exclaiming "Lord, burn eternity into our eyeballs!" This vision is exactly what the church and its servants so desperately need today. The oft-quoted proverb, "He's so heavenly minded that he's no earthly good," is simply *not* true. One may be so pious, or so religious, or so mystical, that he is of no earthly use. But not heavenly minded! In fact, it is just the opposite—as the lives of Augustine and Luther and Wesley and Wilberforce and Booth so powerfully attest.

The supreme proof is the swashbuckling, activist life of the Apostle Paul, which was charged and fed by his singularly grand vision of heaven. Paul's own words tell us that his vision of heaven was so vivid that he is not sure whether he was in his body or not, but there he heard "inexpressible things, things that man is not permitted to tell" (2 Corinthians 12:4). And it was this vision that supported him as he stood tall before Jewish princes and Roman magistrates across the Roman Empire and endured an amazing litany of abuses and hardships unique in the annals of history (2 Corinthians 11:23-28). Paul's heavenly mindedness made him of immense earthly good! Fellow servants, it is the same for us. If we will yield to the demands of heaven's reality, and fix our minds on the eternal, we will be of great earthly use wherever we are.

We are to live in the reality of heaven and in anticipation of the day when we shall see him. "But our citizenship is in heaven. And we eagerly await a Savior from there, the Lord Jesus Christ, who, by the power that enables him to bring everything under his control, will transform our lowly bodies so that they will be like his glorious body" (Philippians 3:20-21). We ought to pray as Joe Bayly did in his *Psalm of Anticipation:*

> *Lord Christ*
> *Your servant*
> *Martin Luther*
> *said he only had*
> *two days*
> *on his calendar*
> *today*

and that day
and that's
what I want too.
And I want
to live
today
for
that day.[13]

PART FOUR

HELPS

SIXTEEN

How the Pastor's Wife Can Help

Kent and I have often wondered what would have become of us if my response to him that crucial night had not been one of faith. What if, instead of offering him my faith, I took the part of Job's wife, agreed that the ministry was a cruel joke, and urged him to give it up? Or, as is more common, what if I had been dragging my feet, complaining about our lot in the ministry? In either case he would have felt a bitter justification in quitting. And no amount of backpedaling on my part would have reversed his decision. Kent and I are convinced that if my response had not been one of faith, we would probably not be in the pastorate today. Perhaps, like so many, we would be attempting to insulate our wounded hearts with possessions and hobbies.

What I learned through this incident has stayed with me and served me well in my role as a pastor's wife. But I had not always understood what it really meant to be a pastor's wife.

A New Identity
When my husband was in seminary preparing for the pastorate, I had no idea what I was getting into. I didn't know where to begin, so I started simply by buying the right mayonnaise.

On the third Tuesday night of each month, while Kent

studied and cared for the baby, I attended the Seminary Wives' Auxiliary. At one of the meetings, a revered pastor's wife recommended Hellman's mayonnaise, saying, "Women, mayonnaise is no place to cut corners!" And she was right. It's great stuff. But the fact that simple household hints stayed with me, while the broader spiritual counsel of these godly women did not, reflects on my frame of reference at the time. My experience was simply too limited for me to fully appreciate and apply their advice. Over the course of my marriage and ministry, I have learned that there is a lot more to being a pastor's wife than buying the right mayonnaise.

It has taken years for me to understand the importance of my role as a pastor's wife. There is much confusion today about this because popular culture has invaded the church, suggesting that whole people must establish an identity separate from their spouses. Thus, to be identified as "merely" your husband's wife suggests you have not achieved full personhood. The idea that a woman might actually be fulfilled by the challenge of living life in a supportive role is equated with inferiority.

Here, above everything else, I discovered that a pastor's wife is exactly that, *a wife*. Far from being an inferior role, my place in Kent's life is select. No one else on earth is in this God-ordained position. It startled and refreshed me to realize that Kent needed me as this. He didn't need me to be his buddy, or his counselor, or even his co-pastor. He needed exactly what God had provided him with—a wife. Paul speaks of this mystical relationship in Ephesians 5:31-32: "For this reason a man will leave his father and mother and be united to his wife, and they will become one flesh. This is a profound mystery—but I am talking about Christ and the church."

The mystery is one of intimacy. Marriage is a union so profound that Christ chose it above all other earthly relationships to indicate his relationship to the church. When Kent shared his doubts and fears with me, his wife, he was sharing with his own flesh. The exchange was far more dynamic than if he shared them with a professional counselor or even a loving parent or friend. Because we were one, our power of understanding and insight and influence over each other was wondrously enormous. Kent needed me to be a wife; as such, I could help him in a way open to no one else.

Before woman was ever created, her function was clearly defined. She was described as "a helper suitable for him" (Genesis 2:18). The concept of the female helping the male is exalted by God.

The Incarnate Son of God beautifully demonstrated that all of us are to be servants (John 13). Later, when he was comforting his disciples with the promise of the Holy Spirit, he referred to him as "another Helper" (John 14:16, NASB). By addressing him (the Third Person of the Godhead) as a helper, he forever elevated the position of the one who *assists*. As we trace the Holy Spirit's actions through the New Testament, we find him repeatedly encouraging, comforting, coming alongside, and helping. The work of the Holy Spirit, the Helper, is beautiful! And women are never more lovely than when they follow his example, cherishing their function as helper. There is no better word to describe the role of a pastor's wife than this—helper. It is not demeaning and we must not despise it. It is divine.

My Husband Needed My Help

Years before, when we started out in ministry, our goal was pure and simple: to love and serve God. But, as we so painfully discovered, it is not a simple task. We personally came to realize that the world, the flesh, and the devil mightily war against those who pursue this elevated goal. When Kent that night blurted out, "God is not good," how the darkness must have rejoiced. It was a complete denial of our original goal! My whole being was in alarm. I had to help. But how?

Let me say first what I did not do. I did not attempt to mother Kent or give him pity. Neither did I attempt to come up with a scheme to make the church grow and thus save Kent's "ministry" and preserve God's reputation. Certainly I was tender and sympathetic and participated in the problem-solving and creative thinking. But a wife who allows her husband to wallow in self-pity or attempts to take over and solve things more often contributes to her husband's loss of self-respect, and even effects a subtle emasculation.

The first thing I did was *pray*—really pray. I prayed earnestly, as James recommends (5:16-17), with all my heart and soul, that God would help my husband. My prayers were mixed with tears. I also prayed in detail, bringing every possible aspect of the problem before God. And I prayed constantly—when I did the dishes, while doing the laundry, while driving as part of the carpool, and as I drifted off to sleep. I prayed the words of *Scripture*, personalizing it by inserting Kent's name in many of the passages, especially Ephesians 1:18-19:

> I pray that the eyes of Kent's heart may be enlightened, so that he may know what is the hope of his calling, the riches of his glorious inheritance in the saints, and God's incomparably great power for us who believe.

I listened. I listened patiently to what my husband was saying as long as he wanted to talk. Moreover, I tried to listen intelligently, reading between the lines. As we all know, listening is often described as the most important aspect of communication. Listening is one of my husband's strengths, but he needed to be listened to himself. I also listened well to what others were saying. All of this made me more thoughtful and direct in my prayer.

I asked questions. Why is this important to you? What do we want out of life? What are we here for? I could not know Kent's motives, but I could urge him to consider what they might be. The point of this, of course, was to take him back to basic principles.

I remembered. When alone with my husband, I would purposely recall God's past provision for us. We have a natural tendency to forget the great things God has done for us, as seventy-two verses of Psalm 78 so mournfully chronicle. So we must make a studied effort to remember his goodness. That is why, for example, God commanded Joshua to set up stones of remembrance in Gilgal after the miraculous crossing of the Jordan: "Each of you is to take up a stone on his shoulder, according to the number of the tribes of the Israelites, to serve as a sign among you. In the future, when your children ask you, 'What do these stones mean?' tell them that the flow of the Jordan was cut off before the ark of the covenant of the Lord. When it crossed the Jordan, the waters of the Jordan were cut off. These stones are to be a memorial to the people of Israel forever" (Joshua 4:5-8). As I recalled God's care in the past, I was better able to trust him for the future, and so did Kent.

I read the Scriptures. When life is in disarray, one can easily be tempted to neglect this discipline. It is too easy to become busy setting things right. Besides, it is sometimes difficult to concentrate on what the Word says when the mind is upset and distracted. But I kept myself in the Word, concentrating on its promises. David said, "Your word is a lamp to my feet and a light for my path" (Psalm 119:105) and "I remember your ancient laws, O Lord, and I find comfort in them" (Psalm 119:52). David is right.

I maintained a sense of humor. I like to laugh, as my family well attests. In fact, they often tease me about it. I am an unabashed, enthusiastic fan of Erma Bombeck, and with good reason. For, as Norman Cousins has shown in his book, *Anatomy of an Illness,* humor is essential to our well-being. It is really no laughing matter. It was important that my husband laugh, and even laugh at himself. Laughter brings relief, and laughter at oneself means that one has, in that moment, been able to step back and see his situation from a different perspective. My laughter and the laughter of our children brought health to both of us. "A cheerful heart is good medicine, but a crushed spirit dries up the bones" (Proverbs 17:22).

I verbally encouraged my husband. The word for the ultimate helper, the Holy Spirit, is *Paraclete.* This word consists of two parts, the first meaning to come alongside, and the second to speak or exhort. Solomon says, "A word aptly spoken is like apples of gold in settings of silver" (Proverbs 25:11). Thus I looked for opportunities to give sincere encouragement. This was not very difficult, because I believed in God and in my husband.

I made home and family a priority. During stressful times, some put family priorities on hold. This is a huge mistake. Such neglect will eventually heighten the strain. In keeping things running smoothly at home by staying on top of the children's needs, keeping a neat home, preparing enjoyable family dinners, and involving my husband in days off at the beach, celebrating birthdays, and attending school programs, home remained for him a place of joy and refuge rather than an added source of stress. I cannot overstate how important this was and is.

A New Goal
When the crisis was over and we were well on the way to recovery, I sat down one day and asked myself this question: What do I want to accomplish as a pastor's wife? As I type the answer, it comes from the very sheet of paper upon which I wrote it down twelve years ago. My goal remains the same today: To one day hear God say to Kent, "Well done, good and faithful servant, enter into the joy of your Master." Kent started well; I want him to end well.

I determined to do four things as a means to that end:
First, encourage his love for God. As we have already said

in chapter 4, the number one priority in life is loving God. The Scriptures reveal that among God's moral attributes are goodness, mercy, faithfulness, grace, holiness, and love. But human nature sometimes begins to question these when under trial, and love for God falters. My hope for my husband and myself is that difficult circumstances will never dampen our belief in these attributes, and thus our love for God. My prayer for us is that we will rest in God's character and love him. As William Cowper wrote:

> *Ye fearful saints, fresh courage take;*
> *The clouds ye so much dread*
> *Are big with mercy, and shall break*
> *In blessings on your head.*
>
> *Judge not the Lord by feeble sense,*
> *But trust him for his grace*
> *Behind a frowning providence*
> *He hides a smiling face.*
>
> *Blind unbelief is sure to err,*
> *And scan his work in vain;*
> *God is his own interpreter,*
> *And he will make it plain.*

God is good and worthy of our love. Loving him is the most important thing in life.

Second, encourage him to love truth. Regarding the importance of true thinking about the attributes of God, A. W. Tozer wrote:

> I think it might be demonstrated that almost every heresy that has afflicted the church through the years has arisen from believing about God things that are not true, or from over-emphasizing certain true things so as to obscure other things equally true. To magnify any attribute to the exclusion of another is to head straight for one of the dismal swamps of theology; and yet we are all constantly tempted to do just that.[1]

What Tozer says is right, and it underlines the importance of pastors thinking truly in all areas. A seemingly minor departure from the truth can have massive implications down the line. Moreover, the Scriptures do not speak kindly about those who mislead God's people: "But if anyone causes one of these little ones who believe in me to sin, it would be better for him to have a large millstone hung around his neck and to be drowned in the depths of the sea" (Matthew 18:6). Assuming the position of a teacher of truth brings this solemn warning, "Not many of you should presume to be teachers, my brothers, because you know that we who teach will be judged more strictly" (James 3:1). Truth and the integrity to teach and live it is of the greatest importance. In this day of gurus and fad theologies, we must pray for our husbands to be men of truth.

Third, encourage him to be a man of principle. This means more than having principles—it means sticking to them. My husband is a man of principle. But, for the sake of illustration, what if, in pursuit of greater numbers, he had contradicted his principles and raffled off a Cadillac on Sunday night to get people into church? The community center wouldn't have held all the people! But with such a "success" after only a *small* infraction of his principles, who knows what could be next? We must encourage our husbands never to compromise their principles.

Finally, help him evaluate his success from a biblical perspective. Regardless of what messages Kent receives regarding his work, whether affirming or negative, whether praise or criticism, I encourage him to return again and again to the guidelines of Scripture for self-evaluation. For it is only there, in God's Word, that he can guard against succumbing to either discouragement or arrogance. The road that Christ walked is narrow. It is neither self-deprecating nor self-promoting—it isn't self-centered at all! It is God-centered.

When we are young and idealistic, life stretches before

us with seemingly endless possibilities. As mid-life approaches, and with it the dawning reality of life's transience, it is essential that we *continue* to think like Christians, evaluating our success from an eternal perspective. If we do this, then when we are old and our hair has turned white we will not be full of regrets but full of grace. Our eyes will be soft and kind and eager, knowing that it won't be long until they behold our reward, the Lord Jesus himself.

After having clearly defined my goal, I started praying a new prayer. It is my Sunday morning prayer. Each Sunday, when my husband steps into the pulpit, I pray:

> Dear Lord Jesus,
> I pray that as Kent steps into the pulpit, he will have a keen sense of the heavy responsibility he bears in leading these people. May his desire be, above all else, to communicate what it is you would have us know from your Word this morning. Keep him in truth and may all thoughts of his performance, or the approval of man, be far from him. Amen.

A New Determination

Our experience is important because it brought my husband so close to tragically quitting his calling. As Kent has already stated, people today sometimes make light of such a call. Nevertheless, it is *divinely* real. And I respect his call; I believe in it. So I have determined by God's grace, I will do nothing that would deter him from fulfilling it. This has not always been easy.

When Eve was tempted in the garden, it was the lust of the flesh, the lust of the eye, and the boastful pride of life that enticed her. Nothing has changed. Sometimes I desire an easier, quieter life. Sometimes I long to be free from other people's problems. There are times when I think I would be happier with more things. And there is the constant bombardment of voices telling me that I shouldn't be content apart from more personal power and prestige. But it is foolish thinking. A wise woman once told me that today's woman in search of equality often overlooks the one thing she needs most—an equality of commitment to know God and to obey his voice. The fact is, if she shares this commitment with her husband, a pastor's wife has all she needs to lead a fulfilling and challenging life.

Our life together following the call of God, though it hasn't been trouble-free, has been extremely rewarding. Our mutual commitment to God's call has enabled us to experience a profound unity—something rare and beautiful in this broken world.

SEVENTEEN

How the Congregation Can Help

The wife of a close pastor friend of ours enjoys telling how she awoke one night to find her husband asleep on his elbows and knees at the foot of the bed. His arms were cupped before him as if he were embracing the base of a tree, and he was muttering.

"George! What on earth are you doing?" she cried.

"Shhh," he answered, still asleep. "I'm holding a pyramid of marbles together, and if I move, it's going to tumble down. . . ."

A classic pastor's dream! First, because it was the subconscious revelation of a pressured parson. Second, because the pyramid of marbles is an apt metaphor for a pastor's work.

The pastor's inevitable knowledge of the forces at work among his people—the individual sins of some, the hidden family problems, the conflicts between members, the dissatisfactions, the life-style inconsistencies, the differing perspectives on what the church should be—can make the pastor *feel* as if one wrong move will bring the whole thing down. This feeling is not a sign of weakness, nor is it new to the church. It is typical of the heart that cares.

What is it like to be a pastor? What can a congregation do to help him and encourage his success?

Understand Your Pastor

As we try to understand something of what it is like to be a pastor, we must realize several things: First, the following are generalizations, and no one pastor experiences or feels all that is here described. Second, the following is descriptive of a serious, hardworking pastor who is trying to do his best. We're not talking about ministerial dilettantes or sluggards here. Third, what follows emphasizes the "heavy" side of pastoral experience (when the arms are supporting the pyramid), and must be balanced by what has already been said about the joys and supreme privilege of the call in chapter 12.

Your pastor's calling is uniquely absorbing. A minister's calling is naturally absorbing precisely because it *is* a call. He did not choose his vocation, however willingly he pursued it. Rather, he was chosen for the vocation. Therefore, he does not regard his ministry as simply a job.

A pastoral colleague once quipped, when asked how he was doing, "Things could be worse; I could be doing this for a living!" thus making cheerful reference to the fact that his was not a job but a calling. A dedicated pastor cannot, and dare not, approach his calling as a nine-to-five proposition, or even a career. God's call is upon all his life. It is impossible for him to separate his calling from the rest of his life as is possible in some professions. A divine call to ministry demands absorption.

The call is further absorbing because the pastor regularly deals with life-and-death issues. Other professions may require one to focus on the outcome of a business transaction, an athletic contest, or even the diagnosis of a disease. But the outcome of the pastor's preaching and counseling can mean, humanly speaking, life and death for eternal souls. This reality alone requires vast concentration. And more, it is compounded by the intensely personal nature of pastoral work; so much of it is eye to eye and heart to heart.

Then there is the time factor that further promotes absorption. No dedicated pastor, regardless of the size of his congregation, can do his job in a forty-hour week. To begin with, if he takes his preaching seriously (which he must!) it will require nearly half that time. My own schedule requires a twenty-five hour commitment, though I have been preaching for years. In a forty-hour week, that leaves fifteen hours for prayer, counseling, administration, staff meeting, visitation, and emergencies. A total impossibility! By definition a shepherd's time is not his own. He must always be available for the unexpected. Furthermore, most pastors of smaller churches do not have enough office help, so they find their time diverted from their main pastoral responsibilities.

The time-consuming nature of the pastoral calling, coupled with the fact that it is a divine call that deals with life-and-death issues on an intimate, personal level, makes the ministry uniquely absorbing. This in turn, presents great dangers to the pastor.

Foremost among the dangers is that *he takes himself too seriously.* Some preachers, though thankfully not so many today, fall into this error. Spurgeon once characterized them as having their neckties twisted around their souls.[1] They are the doleful parsons whom novelists delight to caricature. A helpful pastoral epigram here is: *While we cannot take our work seriously enough, we must never take ourselves too seriously.* The Master's servants are at best clay pots—cracked, at that!

Another similar danger is the *messiah complex.* This is seen in the pastor who is so engrossed in his work that he imagines nothing can be done right without him. He is the ubiquitous preacher, present at every committee meeting, presiding at every function, a voice on legs. He has lost touch with the liberating truth that he is expendable.

An allied danger of ministerial absorption is *a preoccupied soul.* Such a minister's mind is always somewhere else. He faces you when you speak, but he always seems to be looking past you. It is an ugly trait.

The classic symptom of pastoral absorption is *overwork*. He puts everything into his work and thinks that he is justified in doing so. And the tragic result of such absorption is neglect of family.

We say all of this because the congregation must realize that absorption is endemic to the pastoral call. One cannot be a good pastor without it, but unchecked it can ruin him. The congregation wishing to understand its pastor and help promote his success must understand this and take proper steps to assist him, as we will later see.

The Difficulty of Your Pastor's Calling

In 1925, when Karl Barth was offered the church of Neumunster near Zurich, Switzerland, he remembered his previous pastorate and demurred:

> I am troubled by the memory of how greatly, how yet more greatly, I failed finally as a pastor of Safenwil. . . . The prospect of having to teach children again, of having to take hold of all kinds of practical problems . . . is really fearful to me.[2]

Karl Barth, whom many (though they may take issue with his theology) consider to be the greatest theological mind of the twentieth century, found the pastorate to be terribly difficult.

Likewise, William Barclay, professor of New Testament at Glasgow and well-known popularizer of biblical scholarship, wrote candidly of his memories:

> I began by being the pastor of a congregation. I can honestly say that that part of my work was the most difficult and exhausting that I ever had to do . . . it was also the most humiliating, in that it could have been done so much better.[3]

Thus two men, whose names today are veritable household words among pastors and students, testify to the difficulty of the pastoral ministry, publicly affirming what all pastors know from their experience.

Why is the pastorate so challenging and difficult? *Because it is opposed by Satan.* The devil hates Christ, his church, and those who lead it. And because of this, church leaders are regularly subjected to special attention from his demonic hosts. This is especially true if one's ministry shows particular spiritual progress. There is a diabolical wisdom coordinating the forces of evil that makes ministers inevitable targets for difficulty. Every congregation must understand this and accordingly pray for their pastors if they wish them to succeed.

But apart from this fundamental spiritual reason for ministerial difficulty there is also a natural reason, namely, that *the pastorate demands that one do so many things well.* The pastor is called to be a competent leader, administrator, counselor, and preacher all at the same time. This may not seem daunting from the outside, but from within it is formidable.

To begin with, the pastor functions as the chief executive officer of a *volunteer* organization! No one, except his secretary and his assistant (if he has either), is compelled to do anything he says. His situation would prove impossible for a business-world CEO, whose wish is his subordinates' command. The pastor cannot lead by command but must lead by example and influence. And if at any point a parishioner disagrees, he can tell his CEO what he thinks and walk out or form an opposition movement. This functional egalitarianism makes leadership a most delicate art.

This is compounded by the fact that the church, so simple to the uninformed, is an immensely complex structure. The church, though the names of the boards and committees will vary, will normally have separate boards of elders, deacons, missions, and education, which in turn will have a welter of standing and ad hoc committees. The hierarchical structure may look good on paper, but the daily functioning will reveal a web of confusion of responsibilities and territorial breeches that would tax the diplomacy of Benjamin Franklin.

Not only must the pastor lead a complex volunteer organization, he must also be a skilled personal counselor. In more than twenty years of ministerial counseling, I have dealt with just about every sin and problem conceivable. I can no longer be shocked. The idea of a naive pastor is a laughable myth. It is doubtful if a professional psychologist has confronted things any more complex and bizarre than I. And as any counselor will tell you, such counseling is intensely draining. There are psychologists who will book no more than fifteen hours of counseling per week because of the emotional stress. Most pastors have several hours of counseling in their weekly schedules! And because sins often affect other members of the congregation and the sociology of sin can extend back for years, pastoral counseling can be even more stressful. Counseling is a major element in making the pastorate difficult.

But perhaps the greatest challenge in pastoring is preaching. This first issues from the huge responsibility one bears in preaching the Word. C. H. Spurgeon gave eloquent testimony to this when he said:

> It may be light work to you men of genius and learning; but to me it is life and death work. Often have I thought that I would rather take a whipping with a cat-o'-nine-tails than preach again. How can I answer for it at the last great day unless I am faithful? "Who is sufficient for these things?" When I have felt the dread responsibility of souls that may be lost or saved by the word they hear . . . [it] made me wish that I had never ventured on so bold a life-work. How shall I give an honorable account of my commission at last?[4]

For Spurgeon and anyone else who sees the greatness of the responsibility, preaching becomes difficult because it can never be good enough.

In this connection, preaching is difficult because it demands the best of the preacher. Uncovering the exegetical meaning of a text in its context can take hours of work; giving the central idea of the text sermonic shape takes even more hours; applying and illustrating it, still more. And then, even if the preacher is St. Augustine, the sermon may not measure up. "My preaching," said Augustine, "almost always displeases me."[5]

Not least among the challenges of preaching is that the pastor speaks to the same people week after week. In awe of this, John Bright, the famous English statesman and orator, said, "Nothing that I can think of would induce me to undertake to speak to the same audience once a week for a year!"[6] Nevertheless, God calls his pastors to do it once, and often twice or three times a week. Any congregation that has sat under a pastor for several years has heard just about all his "silver bullets," favorite stories, anecdotes, and illustrations. The challenge of preaching to the same people increases with time!

Finally, preaching is intrinsically difficult because of the self-exposure it entails. Phillips Brooks, the redoubtable preacher of turn-of-the-century Boston, said, "Preaching is God's truth mediated through personality."[7] Brooks was stressing the necessity that the preacher internalize the truth and then present it through his own experience. Ultimately this involves some exposure and pain. Bruce Thieleman puts it this way:

> The pulpit calls those anointed to it as the sea calls its sailors; and like the sea, it batters and bruises, and does not rest. . . . To preach, to really preach, is to die naked a little at a time and to know each time that you must do it again.[8]

This is not to say that preaching is an onerous task. Far from it—it is a glorious calling! Rather, it is to stress that preaching is a uniquely difficult task because it is so personal, so time-consuming, and such a vast responsibility.

Any congregation that cares about understanding its pastor must understand and *believe* that the ministry is uniquely difficult; first, because the pastor is a special target of Satan's opposition; and second, because he is called to do so many required things well—lead a *volunteer* organization, give discerning counsel, and preach God's holy Word. In this connection, the congregation must believe that the pastorate is work. Every pastor has heard a variation of this line innumerable times—"What's it like to work one day a week?" It is almost always a good-natured, playful remark and should be regarded as such. But it also voices the common folklore (no doubt deserved by some) that the pastorate is a soft job.

A young teenage girl once asked Barbara, "What does Mr. Hughes do?"

"You know, Suzi," Barbara replied, "he's pastor of College Church."

"Yes, but what does he do the rest of the week?" My wife suggested that she go ask her parents, who were missionaries!

The bottom line, in terms of understanding your pastor, is that the difficult nature of his job makes him a likely candidate for stress. Moreover, if he does not learn how to cope with the pressures of his work, his divine calling can tragically bring harm to both him and his congregation.

But, happily, there are things that both he and his people can do to avoid this, as we shall see.

The Vulnerability of Your Pastor
C. S. Lewis wrote in *The Four Loves:*

> To love at all is to be vulnerable. Love anything, and your heart will certainly be wrung and possibly be broken. If you want to make sure of keeping it intact, you must give your heart to no one, not even to an animal. Wrap it carefully round with hobbies and little

luxuries; avoid all entanglements; lock it up safe in the casket or coffin of your selfishness. But in that casket—safe, dark, motionless, airless—it will change. It will not be broken; it will become unbreakable, impenetrable, irredeemable. The alternative to tragedy, or at least to the risk of tragedy, is damnation. The only place outside heaven where you will be perfectly safe from all dangers and perturbations of love is hell.[9]

Certainly Lewis is right. The greater one's love, the greater one's vulnerability. And for the Christian especially, a safe, insulated life is not an option, because a Christian is commanded to love (Mark 12:30-31). This is emphatically true for the pastor, because he is charged with an official love relationship with his congregation. By giving himself to his people in ministry and involving himself in their lives, he multiplies his vulnerability. This is no sacrifice, because love normally begets love (1 John 4:19). But it does make the pastor's heart vulnerable to a sea of sorrows from which an unloving heart is safe. When one of his flock hurts, he hurts; when one is bereaved, he is bereaved; when one backslides, he agonizes. As Paul says: "Who is weak, and I do not feel weak? Who is led into sin, and I do not inwardly burn?" (2 Corinthians 11:29). It is a privileged vulnerability because it is a vulnerability to joy as well as sorrow; for as Paul also says, his beloved brethren are his joy (Philippians 4:1). The pastor is profoundly vulnerable because of his office. This must be believed by those who would understand him.

The pastor is not only vulnerable because of involvement with his people, he is also vulnerable because he leads a public life. Though it is not nearly as intense as it was in past decades, the pastor and his family still lead a fishbowl existence. Almost everything the pastor does can be scrutinized by church people—selection of house and cars, tastes in clothing, choice of entertainments and vacations—to name a few possibilities. This fishbowl syndrome has given rise to the circulation among pastors of some inside humor about the "Ideal Pastor":

The Ideal Pastor:
is always casual but never underdressed—
is warm and friendly but not too familiar—
is humorous but not funny—
calls on his members but is never out of the office—
is an expository preacher but always preaches on the family—
is profound but comprehensible—
condemns sin but is always positive—
has a family of ordinary people who never sin—
has two eyes, one brown and the other blue!

This overdrawn parody gives expression to the vulnerability all have felt at one time or another. And this fishbowl factor can have a debilitating effect on the pastor, especially if his family senses that it is under the microscope.

Another similar hazard of being the focus of public attention is that it can open one to irrational hostility. That happens through *transference.* Someone may be suffering intense anxiety or anger over a personal problem, possibly an illness or a professional conflict, but there is no safe outlet for the anxiety. So a *safe* subconscious transference is made to the church or the pastor. This can be destructive emotionally and sometimes even physically.

Finally, we must mention that the pastor is vulnerable simply because he is human. Despite his pressed suit and starched shirt and his weekly ecclesiastical air of wholeness, he is a sinner who wrestles with his temper and self-discipline. He has his dreams, foibles, and blind spots. He has insecurities and irrationalities.

In short, the pastorate increases one's vulnerability because, though it is a divine calling, it is intensely human and public. But most of all, it increases vulnerability because it is a calling to love God and man—and to love at all is to be vulnerable.

The Onslaught of the Success Syndrome

Pastor Brown had served First Church for fifteen wonderful years. During those years the church had experienced slow but steady growth. It had become a rather large church of more than a thousand. The pastor was grateful for the growth and looked forward to more. But numbers had never been Pastor Brown's thing. He liked to preach, was a good preacher, and sometimes was invited away to speak. But he best enjoyed being with his people and involved in their lives. He had performed so many marriages that he had lost count, and it was the same with funerals. Only he never forgot the people. Many in the church owed the health of their marriages to his prayer and counsel. Missions was his special joy. Most of First's missionaries had gone out under his ministry. Pastor Brown was a man who loved his people and was loved by them.

He had no reason to expect what was coming. It began when several executives of a large corporation became elders. Their energy and interest in First Church's ministry was refreshing, though sometimes Pastor Brown sensed their shared impatience. The bombshell came over a business lunch with one of the men. "Pastor, several of the elders and I have been discussing your future with First Church—and let me be frank—we do not think you're the man to take us into the next decade. In our business, we are expected to show a designated percentage growth per year. We've done some research, and in the light of the demographics, First Church ought to be growing 10 percent annually. Under your leadership it's been between 2 and 4 percent. In our opinion, your style is excellent for a shepherd, but what First Church needs is a rancher."

And so it began. The people wanted Pastor Brown, but the leadership did not. It was too much for the pastor. Infighting was not his style, and there had already been some innocent casualties. After two years of struggle, Pastor Brown, a man faithful and hardworking, one who loved and served God with a servant's heart, a man of prayer and holiness, a person whose attitude was upbeat and positive, resigned. The quantifiers had their day. First Church has never been the same.

Tragically, Pastor Brown's experience is not unique, for secularized ideals of success, straight from the business world, are increasingly being applied in the church. A church must "turn a profit," so to speak. Thus, whatever else can be positively said about a church, it is not succeeding unless it is growing numerically. Big, growing churches are, by definition, the most successful. In some instances, a secularized competitiveness grips the church. If Second Church outgrows First, it is more successful. And, in some, like Pastor Brown's church, a cold quantity-based pragmatism is in the driver's seat.

How does this affect the pastor? Incredible as it may sound, he is treated differently according to the size of his church. This may be expected in the business world, but not in the church! I well remember the change that took place when I went from a small to a large church: how a new light of recognition came to people's eyes when I was introduced and how my opinions became more cogent and important. Respect, it seems, is proportionate to the size of one's ministry.

This means that there are untold numbers of pastors whose self-worth is affected by the size of their churches. This means that many pastors of smaller churches feel discouraged and insecure. In a word, this means *pressure*.

Your pastor's situation, his disposition, and his maturity will determine how much pressure he feels. But it is there. Believe it, if you wish to understand him. The unhappy goddess of secular success is taking its toll in the church.

All Those Marbles
Every pastor has times when he feels as if he is holding a mountain of marbles together because the pastorate is an

intrinsically difficult, absorbing, and vulnerable position, and because he is sometimes assaulted by wrong thinking about success.

A congregational understanding of this can go far in encouraging him—*and* keeping all those marbles in place.

We have given lengthy consideration to understanding your pastor because that in itself will ultimately encourage him. A congregation that understands the ministry will support it intelligently and practically. But there are some more specific ways in which a congregation (especially its leadership) can encourage its pastor.

First, you can encourage your pastor by living biblically successful lives yourselves. There is little that will lift the pastoral heart more than people who are successes before God (faithful, serving, loving, believing, praying, holy, and positive), for this means that the fullness of Christ is active in the congregation and that the vision and burden of ministry is being shared. It means that the pastor will have some people around him who are cheerful, hardworking, selfless, and supportive. The heartening effect of this cannot be overemphasized.

But it is more than heartening, for it also encourages the pastor to pursue ideals and programs consonant with true success. The presence of just a few people, even if they are not in leadership, who understand what success is and live it out, will be of immense help to the pastor in keeping his perspective. It is a fact of life that character and ideals are most powerfully communicated from life to life, rather than imposed.

So in encouraging your pastor, the place to begin is with your own heart. As a layperson and not a professional, you perhaps have read the preceding chapters with interest, but without thinking of personal application—much like reading someone else's mail. If so, we must emphasize that the teaching is transferable and applies *in principle* no less to you! And we must ask you: Are you committed to a truly successful Christian life? If not, we suggest that you turn now to the end of chapter 10 where the elements of success are applied, and confirm your commitment before proceeding.

Second, encourage your pastor by your personal commitment to help him know true success. In doing this we are not encouraging self-righteous presumption: "Now pastor, I'm concerned that you be a success. So I've committed myself to help you live out these seven things"—whether *he* likes it or not! Never do anything like this, ever! Such an approach projects a proud, condescending spirit that has sat in judgment on the pastor and found him wanting.

Rather, we recommend that you work out your commitment practically. To begin with, commit yourself to freeing him from a ministry of numbers. This does not mean that numbers have no significance. They do. The Scriptures record that three thousand were converted at Pentecost (Acts 2:41) and that Jesus fed five thousand (Mark 14:21). Numbers of souls saved and ministered to are important. They are substantive causes for rejoicing, because they indicate that the gospel touched many. But, as we have seen, numbers do not mean success. In point of fact, if only three had responded at Pentecost and a mere five were fed by Christ, neither would have been less successful.

This does not release the pastor from the significance of attendance as an aspect of the evaluation of ministerial effectiveness, but it does release him from the delusion that numbers mean success. Neither does it mean that the pastor is free from accountability in matters of work habits, administration, creativity, preaching, and even spiritual discipline. Many ministers would profit from the church's caring enough to demand more accountability.

Positively, this means that the church must commit itself to creating an environment in which its pastors are encouraged to be men of God and to pursue biblically defined success. And here, the congregation, apart from being people who understand what success is and live it, can do some specific things to create an encouraging environment, as the next points will show.

Third, encourage your pastor by not expecting (or allowing) him to be involved in everything. Reject the ubiquitous pastor fallacy—that the good minister must be present and presiding, if possible, at everything. Some congregations think that this is what the pastor is for, and apparently many pastors agree, or at least appear to. Such clerics feel it is their duty to attend *all* the meetings of *every* church board and committee, and even conduct a kind of divine shuttle service between those that meet at the same time! They are present and hovering at every church event whether it be volleyball or a bake sale. Every decision must have their imprimatur—from the color of the ladies' powder room to the logo on the baseball uniforms. Such pastors are perspiring, kinetic figures, the only ones who know where anything is from the church records to the kitchen's large saucepan.

This tendency may be the result of pastoral *absorption* brought on by the intense demands of the ministry, or possibly a faulty doctrine of the church that ignores the shared nature of pastoral ministry (see Acts 6:1-6; 1 Corinthians 12; Ephesians 4:11-12). At worst, such behavior may indicate personal insecurity ("My work makes me indispensable"), or a distrust of people (a terribly destructive attitude, though, alas, often founded upon some unhappy ministerial experience in the past).

How should the leadership of the congregation proceed to help the omnipresent pastor? Again the approach must not be officious or heavy-handed but loving and sacrificial—for the congregation must be willing to assume much of the burden. This being so, the pastor can be reminded, if necessary, of what the Scriptures teach and of the church's desire to free him so he can give himself "to prayer and the ministry of the word" (Acts 6:4). The leadership must help him divest himself of the things he does that could, and should, be done by others. The minister should understand which boards and committees he must regularly attend, and those which he should only infrequently visit, say, at the request of the chairpersons. The leadership must insist that as their minister streamlines his schedule, he include ample time for his devotional life, family, sermon preparation, exercise, and leisure.

To be sure, the compulsive pastor may not at first view such concern by the leadership as in his best interest, but if he adjusts his life accordingly, the day will come that he and his family will thank God and the church.

Fourth, encourage your pastor by providing adequately for him and his family. This involves proper salary, vacation, study time, and days off.

Salary. An excellent rule of thumb is that the pastor's salary and benefits should be at a level that is near the median income of the congregation, thus enabling his family to live on the level of the people he ministers to. There are also occasions in which the salary should exceed the median. For example, if the minister is married and the church is largely young singles and students, as is the case in some urban churches, the pastor should, nevertheless, be remunerated at a level at which he can support his family. Moreover, the level should be such that his wife is not forced to work.

Small churches, of course, find it much more difficult to provide for their pastors, and sometimes the pastor must take a second job. In these cases, he must not be expected to be able to do as much as a man who has no extra obligations.

Vacation. Our advice regarding vacations is that churches should begin by granting three weeks instead of the traditional two. Because the ministry is so absorbing, and because most ministers have only one day off per week, there can develop a professional claustrophobia. The best cure for this is a substantial time away. Most ministers find that it takes a week just to unwind—to really believe that they are on vacation. Three weeks is a good place to begin and should be extended to four after a few years of faithful ministry.

Study time. Many churches also provide their pastors with one or two study weeks per year. These are not vacations and cannot be used for "vacation extenders." They are for spiritual and intellectual renewal. To guard their purpose and effectiveness some churches require that the study weeks not be contiguous to vacations and that the minister indicate what he will study.

Days off. Here we must also stress the importance of encouraging the pastor to take a day off. It is not uncommon, because of emergencies and special meetings, for a minister to go two or three weeks without doing so. Help him by gently reminding him that his calling does not cancel his humanity. Encourage him to get away and smell the flowers, or wash the car. Both can be restorative! Insist that he take a couple of back-to-back days away once in awhile.

Burn-out has become epidemic in the ministry. But the church can help forestall this by making wise provision for adequate salary and time away from work.

Fifth, encourage your pastor by loving his family. As we noted earlier, the fishbowl life of the pastoral ministry can take its toll—especially on the pastor's family. Not a few PKs have reacted to the feeling of being under the congregation's microscope. Sometimes the reaction is unfounded, even irrational; other times it has substance. What can the congregation do to minimize this effect? Simply, love his family. By this we are not emphasizing a public display of compassion but a quiet familylike love that recognizes they are people in process like those in one's own family. This love does not demand more from them than from other children; it does not say, "Why you're the pastor's son, I would have expected . . ." This love honors their individuality and gives them space to grow. This love refuses to gossip, believes the best, has a kind word, and prays for the pastor's family.

The congregation will do well to realize that it is likewise under scrutiny by the pastor's family. Children who sense that they are loved rather than judged by the people their father serves will have a greater opportunity to become the kind of young people their family and church hope for. This, of course, brings vast encouragement to the pastor—and the congregation.

Sixth, encourage your pastor by treating him with respect. A pastor should be treated with respect because of his divinely given position. This, of course, does not suggest that he be treated with an obsequious obeisance as some nineteen century clerics were—"His Worshipful Lordship, Rev. Dr. Pangloss. . . ." Nor does it suggest undue deference—"Whatever you say, pastor. . . ." What we mean is that because the pastorate is a divine office, a minister should never have to earn his congregation's respect unless he has done something to lose it. Furthermore, he should be respected no matter how great or small, grand or humble his ministry is! The church must dismiss the world's rung-dropping, numbers-counting way of according respect. True, your pastor is to lead by being a servant, but such a call is intrinsically honored.

This understanding must be extended to churches that have several pastors and multiple staffs. The tendency in large churches is for the people to think of the senior pastor as *the* pastor, and everyone else as almost-pastors. Youth pastors are special victims, for they are sometimes asked by congregants when they are going to become pastors! A huge insult. The implication is that they are something else—possibly zookeepers. Understand that a pastor is a pastor is a pastor regardless of his station, size of ministry, or public exposure, and should be treated with due respect. How so many pastors need this encouragement today!

When the congregation, and especially its leaders, have encouraged the pastor by (1) living biblically successful lives, (2) committing themselves to help him know true success, (3) relieving him of the expectation that he do everything, (4) providing adequately for him and his family, (5) loving his family, and (6) treating him with respect, the church will have done almost everything it can to encourage him—except for the most important thing, which is to pray.

Conclusion

Every pastor knows that the strength of the ministry rests on prayer, and that it is those faithful souls who pray regularly for him and the church who bring God's special blessing upon the ministry. This fact invites a marvelous "what if" scenario. What if not just a few but the entire leadership and congregation prayed *in detail every day* for the pastor and their church? What would happen to his heart, to his preaching, to worship, to evangelism, to missions? Can there be any doubt that the minister and his people would know greater enablement than ever before in their lives?

Prayer is where the congregation must begin in this whole matter of encouragement. Will you make a personal commitment to encourage your pastor by daily prayer for him and his work? If so, we leave you with this suggestive outline, from which you can draw your own prayer list.

Pray that he will be a true success: that he will be *faithful,* true to God's Word and hardworking; that he will be a *servant,* following the example of our foot-washing Lord; that he will *love God* with all his heart, soul, mind, and strength; that he will truly *believe* what he believes about Christ; that he will lead a *holy* life, and not succumb to the sensuality of our culture; that he will lead a life of deep *prayer,* following Jesus' example; that he will have a positive *attitude* free from jealousy.

Pray for his ministry—for his preaching, for time to prepare, for understanding the Word, for application, for the power of the Holy Spirit in delivery, for Sunday's services, for his leadership, for immediate problems he is facing.

Pray for his marriage—for time for each other, for communication, for a deepening love, for fidelity.

Pray for his children by name. Perhaps you might ask the pastor or his wife how they would like you to pray for their children.

The outcome of such detailed daily prayer fosters a compelling vision, but, like success, it is not beyond our reach.

Let us pray for success in the church!

NOTES

Introduction
1. Vernon C. Grounds, "Faith to Face Failure, or What's So Great about Success?" *Christianity Today*, 9 December 1977, 12-13.

Chapter 3
1. Centuries later, as King David lay dying, he called Solomon before him and gave much the same charge, dramatically emphasizing that if he kept God's Word he would have success in all he did and wherever he turned (1 Kings 2:2–3). David's classic expression of this truth is found in the opening lines of the first Psalm, where the man who delights in the law, meditating on it day and night, experiences profound success.
2. A. T. Robertson, *Types of Preachers in the New Testament* (George H. Doran, 1922), 15.
3. William Gordon Blaikie, *The Book of Joshua* (A. C. Armstrong and Son, 1903), 67.
4. E. M. Baldwin, *Henrietta Mears and How She Did It* (Ventura, Calif.: Regal, n.d.), 148.
5. This was said by Billy Graham at the Congress on Discipleship and Evangelism (CODE '76), a gathering of fifteen hundred young people during the Greater San Diego Billy Graham Crusade, August 1976.
6. Elisabeth Elliot, "The Glory of God's Will," *World Vision* magazine, April 1977, 12-13. Also available in booklet form (Westchester, Ill.: Good News Pubs.).

Chapter 4
1. Richard Collier, *The General Next to God* (Glasgow: Collins, 1965), 72.
2. Leon Morris, *The Gospel According to John* (Grand Rapids: Eerdmans, 1971), 616.
3. C. K. Barrett, *The Gospel According to St. John* (London: S.P.C.K., 1975), 366-367.

4. John G. Stackhouse, Jr., "The Gospel Song" (an unpublished parody).

5. Robert A. Raines, *Creative Brooding* (New York: Macmillan, 1966).

Chapter 6

1. Brooke Foss Westcott, *The Epistle to the Hebrews* (New York: Macmillan, 1920), 358, where he says that faith "included two elements, the belief (a) that God is, and (b) that he is morally active; in other words it is a faith in the existence and in the moral government of God."

2. Peter T. O'Brien, *Colossians, Philemon,* vol. 44, in the *Word Biblical Commentary* (Waco, Tex.: Word, 1982), 47, where O'Brien says, "Paul's teaching about Christ as the goal of all creation . . . finds no parallel in the Jewish wisdom literature or in the rest of extant Jewish materials for that matter."

3. H. Dermot McDonald, *Commentary on Colossians and Philemon* (Waco, Tex.: Word, 1980), 49.

4. I. M. Anderson, "When Sankey Sang the Shepherd Song," *Moody Monthly*, February 1986, 77-78.

Chapter 7

1. William D. Boyd, "I Work Too Hard!" *Western Witness*, vol. 14, no. 4 (Morrison, Colo.: Western Bible College).

2. I. D. E. Thomas, *The Golden Treasury of Puritan Quotations* (Chicago: Moody Press), 210.

3. Rolland Hein, ed., *Creation in Christ* (Wheaton, Ill.: Harold Shaw, 1978), 317.

4. E. Stanley Jones, *A Song of Ascents* (Nashville: Abingdon, 1968), 383.

5. Pastor Paul P. Stough, one of my fellow pastors in College Church, a man who previously served forty-eight years in Africa with Africa Inland Mission, gave this account on March 11, 1982.

6. Lois Neely, *Come Up to This Mountain* (Wheaton, Ill.: Tyndale House, 1980), 65.

7. E. M. Bounds, *Power Through Prayer* (Grand Rapids: Zondervan, 1982), 28.

8. Excerpted from the personal correspondence of J. Sidlow Baxter, September 8, 1987.

Chapter 8

1. Numbers 6 further informs us that this was symbolized by three vows. First, they abstained from strong drink. This was a hardship in a land where fermented drinks were normal fare, but it made for a distinctive life in an environment where alcoholism was an extremely serious problem, thus emphasizing the Nazarite's separation to God. God was all the Nazarite needed. Second, the Nazarite refrained from cutting his hair. This vow rose from the emphasis that the Nazarite's entire body and life belonged to God, and if the hair remained untrimmed, it served as a witness

against any who shaved their heads in service of pagan gods. (Geoffrey W. Bromiley, ed., *The International Standard Bible Encyclopedia*, vol. 3, "Nazarite" [Grand Rapids: Eerdmans, 1986], 501-502.) And finally, in the third vow, the Nazarite promised not to come in contact with anything dead and become ceremonially unclean, for he was alive unto God.
2. J. Alberto Soggin, *Judges* (London: SCM Press, Ltd., 1981), 241.
3. J. Allan Petersen, *The Myth of the Greener Grass* (Wheaton, Ill.: Tyndale House, 1983), 29.
4. J. Oswald Sanders, *Bible Men of Faith* (Chicago: Moody Press, 1974), 13.

Chapter 9
1. Frederick Langbridge, *A Cluster of Quiet Thoughts* (London: The Religious Tract Society, 1896), n.p.
2. Henry Fairlie, *The Seven Deadly Sins* (Notre Dame, Ind.: Univ. of Notre Dame Press, 1979), 79.
3. John R. Claypool, *The Preaching Event* (Waco, Tex.: Word, 1980), 68.
4. Hugh Evan Hopkins, *Charles Simeon of Cambridge* (Grand Rapids: Eerdmans, 1977), 111.

Chapter 10
1. Here we must insert some caution, for wrongly applied these questions could promote legalism. Legalism is *self-righteous*. How easily our sinful hearts can subvert positive answers to these questions into self-righteous pride, and thus an unwitting descent from the success we imagine for ourselves. The fact is, no one will perfectly attain to the elements of success as we have described them. These elements are guideposts for the lives of those who desire success. They are meant to keep us on the path, rather than promote the belief that we have arrived.

Legalism is likewise *judgmental*. How naturally we incline to mercilessly apply these questions to others and grade their success. This is something we must never do! None but the hearts that ask these questions of themselves can answer them.

Legalism is also *reductionist*. It reduces the spirituality of the elements of success to wooden laws, and then says, "If you can do these five, or ten, or twenty things you will be a success. God forbid! Biblical success is more than the elements we have discussed.

What we have done thus far is delineate *some* of the obvious distinctives of Biblical success and present them as indicators of where we, as God's children, stand in our pursuit of success. So, as we ask these questions we do not ask them legalistically, but graciously with the hope that God's servants will be delivered from the tyranny of wordly thinking about success to the liberating teaching of God's Word—and know success.

Chapter 11
1. Oswald Sanders, *Spiritual Leadership* (Chicago: Moody Press, 1967), 141.
2. Theodore Laetsch, *Bible Commentary Jeremiah* (St. Louis: Concordia, 1965), 234-235.
3. Malcolm Muggeridge, *A Twentieth Century Testimony* (Nashville: Thomas Nelson, 1978), 35.
4. Joseph Bayly, "The Severity and Goodness of God," *Eternity* (September 1986), 80.
5. Clarence Edward Macartney, *Preaching Without Notes* (Grand Rapids: Baker, 1976), 56-57.

Chapter 12
1. C. E. B. Cranfield, *Romans*, vol. 2 (Edinburgh: T & T Clark, 1975), 603-605, confirms that "reasonable" is still a good rendering of *logikos*, which bears the root idea of logical.
2. See Exod. 3:10–11; 4:10–17; Isa. 6:1–13; Jer. 1:4–10; Acts 9:15–16; 26:16; 1 Cor. 9:16; Matt 28:19–20; Acts 1:8.
3. Wilbur M. Smith, *The Life of Will Houghton* (Grand Rapids: Eerdmans, 1951), 62-63.
4. Warren Wiersbe, *Walking with the Giants* (Grand Rapids: Baker, 1979), 269.
5. Macartney, *Preaching Without Notes*, 10.
6. Iain Murray, *Martyn Lloyd-Jones*, (Carlisle, Pa.: Banner of Truth Trust, 1982), 150.
7. Ray C. Stedman, "Why I Am an Expositor," *Theology, News and Notes* (December 1985), 6-7.
8. Phillips Brooks, *Lectures on Preaching* (Manchester: James Robinson, 1899), 83-84.

Chapter 13
1. "Man's Weakness—God's Strength," *Missionary Crusader* (December 1964), 7.
2. William Barclay, *The Master's Men* (Naperville, Ill.: SCM Book Club, 1959), 41-44.
3. Peter T. O'Brien, *Colossians and Philemon* (Waco, Tex.: Word, 1982), 111, says, "The *essence* of God, undivided and in its whole fullness, dwells in Christ in his exalted state, so that he is the essential and adequate image of God."

Chapter 14
1. The Spurgeon, Jowett, and Whyte illustrations are paraphrased from Wiersbe, *Walking with the Giants*, 263-265.
2. Ibid., 264.
3. Charles Hodge, *An Exposition of the Second Epistle to the Corinthians* (Grand Rapids: Eerdmans, 1953), 10.
4. Phillips Brooks, *The Influence of Jesus* (London: H. R. Allenson, 1895), 191.
5. Wiersbe, *Walking with the Giants*, 264.

Chapter 15
1. Joseph Bayly, *Heaven* (Elgin, Ill.: David C. Cook, 1977), 3, 6.
2. Joseph Bayly, *The Last Thing We Talk About* (Elgin, Ill.: David C. Cook, 1980), 114.
3. Bayly, *Heaven*, 20.
4. Ibid., 40.
5. W. D. Davies, *Paul and Rabbinic Judaism* (London: S.P.C.K., 1955), 307, says, ". . . the language that he used in 1 Cor. 2:9 to describe the blessedness of the Age to Come was evidently traditional in Judaism."
6. Bayly, *The Last Thing We Talk About*, 114-115.
7. James Denny, *The Second Epistle to the Corinthians* (London: Hodder and Stoughton, n.d.), 169.
8. C. K. Barrett, *A Commentary on the Second Epistle to the Corinthians* (London: Adam and Charles Black, 1973), 147.
9. C. S. Lewis, *Transposition and Other Addresses* (Geoffrey Bles, 1949), 21-22.
10. Additional information about rewards can be studied by looking at the passages that refer to rewards as crowns: 1 Corinthians 9:25; Philippians 4:1; 1 Thessalonians 2:19; 2 Timothy 4:8; James 1:12; 1 Peter 5:4; Revelation 2:10-11.
11. See Matthew 25:21 and Revelation 22:3. Bayly, *The Last Thing We Talk About*, 115, remarks,

    Heaven is also a place of activity, of work (but without the curse of toil and sweat and barren ground), of sharing in the responsibility of divine government.
    I sat with a friend in his hospital room. The diagnosis is terminal cancer. If death comes, it will interrupt a distinguished career as a leader in training young men to serve Jesus Christ.
    "When we think of heaven," he said, "I don't think we give enough consideration to what we're told in Revelation, that 'His servants serve Him,' and that their service is 'day and night.' We talk too much about rest—our rest will be found in serving God."

12. Joseph Bayly, "Psalm 29," *Psalms of My Life* (Wheaton, Ill.: Tyndale, 1978).
13. Bayly, "Psalm 26," *Psalms of My Life*.

Chapter 16
1. A. W. Tozer, *The Knowledge of the Holy* (New York: Harper and Row, 1961), 85.

Chapter 17
1. Charles H. Spurgeon, *Lectures to My Students* (Grand Rapids: Zondervan, 1969), 166-167.
2. T. H. L. Parker, *Karl Barth* (Grand Rapids: Eerdmans, 1970), 49.
3. William Barclay, *A Spiritual Biography* (Grand Rapids: Eerdmans, 1975), 49.

4. Charles H. Spurgeon, "Mediator-The Interpreter," *The Metropolitan Tabernacle Pulpit*, vol. 35 (Pilgrim Publications: n.d.), 416.
5. St. Augustine, *On the Catechizing of the Uninstructed*, bk. I, ch. II.3, *The Nicene and Post-Nicene Fathers*, vol. III., ed. Philip Schaff, (Grand Rapids: Eerdmans, 1956), 284.
6. *FocalPoint*, July-September 1986 (Denver Conservative Baptist Seminary).
7. Phillips Brooks, *Lectures on Preaching* (London: H. R. Allenson, 1902), 5.
8. *FocalPoint*, July-September 1986.
9. C. S. Lewis, *The Four Loves* (Geoffrey Bles, 1960), 138-139.